Calculator Maths: Shap

Alan Graham and Barrie Galpin

Published by A+B Books

Texas Instruments Version

Copyright © 1998 Alan Graham and Barrie Galpin.

All rights reserved. No part of this work may be reproduced or transmitted in any form or by any means, electronic or mechanical, including photocopying and recording, or by any information storage or retrieval system, without permission in writing from the publisher.

ISBN 0-9533137-3-5

Cover designed by Jonathan Davies.
Cartoons by Steve Smith.

Printed by Welton Print Limited, 17a Queensway Trading Estate, Leamington Spa, CV31 3LZ.
Telephone 01926 431331

This book is one of five in the **Calculator Maths** series.
The other four are titled:
    Foundations   ISBN 0-9533137-0-0
    Number   ISBN 0-9533137-1-9
    Algebra   ISBN 0-9533137-2-7
    Handling Data   ISBN 0-9533137-4-3

ATTENTION EDUCATIONAL ORGANISATIONS

Quantity discounts are available on bulk purchases of the books in this series.
For information, please contact:
    A+B Books
    15 Top Lodge
    Fineshade
    Near Corby NN17 3BB
    Tel: 01780 444360

A+B Books

Calculator Maths: Shape

Before you start using Calculator Maths: Shape

There are three main types of people who might be reading this. Which type are you?

- Students studying alone.
- Students in school.
- Mathematics teachers.

Whichever of the three you are, **Calculator Maths** will be of use to you only if you have a calculator – and not just any calculator. The books have been produced with Texas Instruments calculators in mind. These are Large Screen Calculators, often called Graphics, or Graphing, or Graphical Calculators. All the screen displays and key-press sequences in the book are based on the TI-80 calculator but if you are using a TI-83 or TI-82 the keys are so consistent that you will get by without any problem.

If you are using another make or model you will need to adapt some of the activities although the ideas and principles can still be applied. If you are a student (either studying alone or in school) you should read the next section before you start using the books.

Students should read this

Will Calculator Maths teach me how to use the calculator?

Yes! **Calculator Maths: Foundations** has been written to provide new users with all the basic calculator skills they are likely to need in the later books. If using this sort of calculator is something which is new to you, you should start by working carefully through the section *Introducing the calculator* in **Foundations**. There are two practice exercises with answers at the back of the book. Also in that book is a reference section, *How-to...* where you can look up particular calculator skills and methods if you need to. There are two other sections towards the end of the book: *Writing your own programs* and *Trouble Shooting*. You don't need to read these until you are ready to do so.

Will I learn maths as well?

Yes! In the other **Calculator Maths** books the emphasis is on learning mathematics using the calculator rather than on the calculator itself.

The other four books deal with topics in **Number**, **Algebra**, **Shape** and **Handling Data**. Each book is made up of units related to its particular theme.

In what order should I study the materials?

You should use this book only after you have worked through *Introducing the calculator* in **Foundations**. You don't need to study the other books or units in any particular order. Each unit consists of a number of *Activities*. Think about that word – you are meant to be active as you do them and that means an active head as well as active fingers! As you do the activity you will be learning and gaining in mathematical understanding.

At the back of the book there are answers and comments. We are sure you'll want to use the answers to check your work, especially if you are a student working alone without a teacher.

© *Alan Graham and Barrie Galpin*

Calculator Maths: Shape

What are the Brain stretchers and the Discussion sections?

Most units also have some *Brain stretchers*. We chose this name with some care! They are optional and usually harder sections which may stretch your brain just that bit further. Does your brain need stretching? – well, you are the best one to know. If you fancy a challenge, try some of these.

At the end of each unit there is a list of points for *discussion* which your teacher may want you to think about. If you are working on your own, you should think about these and make some notes before looking at the comments in the back of the book.

Will using the calculator rot my brain?

Possibly!! You could seriously damage your mental skills if you rely too much on the calculator. But we think that the calculator can actually help you think more deeply as well as being fun – but not if you are mindlessly pushing buttons. There are a number of activities, such as *Guess and Press*, where you are expected to think first and use the calculator to check your answer. If you get it right you can give yourself a mental pat on the back. If you're wrong, no one else will know and there is then a real opportunity to learn something. Of course, you can cheat – but then, what's the point? It's about as pointless as looking up the answers before you've tried the questions!

Teachers should read this

Using Calculator Maths

Calculator Maths has been written so that it can be used alongside your existing maths scheme. After students have worked through *Introducing the calculator* in **Foundations**, they should be able to tackle the units in any order, although on occasions it is advisable to have studied one unit before starting another. In such cases there is a warning to that effect at the beginning of the appropriate section of *Solutions* at the back of the book. Also, within any unit there is a progression of ideas and levels of difficulty so you may wish to pick and choose which activities are appropriate for your students at any particular time.

The assumption throughout the books is that students will have one calculator each. The calculator is essentially a personal tool and although on rare occasions there may be benefits in using one machine as a focus of discussion for two or more students, this is not usually the case.

Solutions

At the beginning of each page of *Solutions* you will find the following notes which will help you as you prepare lessons based around the material.

- A summary of what we consider to be the key ideas of the unit.
- Whether the unit is suitable for use with other TI calculators.
- Whether any previous units need to be studied before this one.
- The new calculator skills introduced in the unit (that is over and above the ones covered in *Introducing your calculator* in **Foundations**).
- What we term mathematical jargon – every *sphere* of life has its own *set* of terms which *count* as having a special meaning and mathematics is a *prime* example of this!

Seeing the bigger picture

Students are often so focused on a specific activity that they fail to look at the bigger picture. It is difficult for them to stand back and ask such questions as; what is the same about all these tasks? what general principle is being demonstrated here? A special feature of the Large Screen Calculator is that it can reduce the burden of calculation and speed up tasks set so that there is time, opportunity and student energy available to reflect on the bigger picture. The discussion sections at the end of each unit, together with the corresponding section in *Solutions*, will provide an opportunity for you, the teacher, to help students reflect upon the specific activities and to move from the particular to the general.

© Alan Graham and Barrie Galpin

Calculator Maths: Shape

Contents of this book:

Calculator Maths: Shape

	Before you start using Calculator Maths: Shape	Page 2
Unit 1	Perimeters and areas	6
2	Volumes	10
3	Pythagoras' theorem	14
4	Sin, cos and tan	18
5	Similar shapes	22
6	Locus	26
7	Polygons	30
8	Circles	34
9	Transforming shapes	38
	Solutions	42

Contents of the other books in the series:

Calculator Maths: Foundations

Before you start using Calculator Maths	Page 2
Introducing the calculator	6
How-to...	30
Writing your own programs	44
Trouble shooting	50
Solutions	54

© Alan Graham and Barrie Galpin

Calculator Maths: Number

Unit 1	Rounding	Page 6
2	Squares and square roots	10
3	Powers and roots	14
4	Standard form	18
5	Equivalent fractions	22
6	Calculating with fractions	26
7	Integers and decimals	30
8	Percentages	34
9	Negative numbers	38
10	Converting units	42
11	Order of operations	46
12	Factors	50

Calculator Maths: Algebra

Unit 1	Letters for numbers	Page 6
2	Sequences	10
3	Formulas and number patterns	14
4	Plotting coordinates	18
5	Straight lines	22
6	Tables of values	26
7	Simple equations	30
8	Inequalities	34
9	Simultaneous equations	38
10	Quadratic equations	42
11	Harder equations	46

Calculator Maths: Handling Data

Unit 1	Random numbers	Page 6
2	Random simulations	10
3	Probability	14
4	Making sense of data lists	18
5	Frequency data	22
6	Summarising data - averages	26
7	Summarising data - spread	30
8	Bar charts and histograms	34
9	Line graphs	38
10	Boxplots	42
11	Scatter diagrams	46
12	Lines of best fit	50

© Alan Graham and Barrie Galpin

Calculator Maths: Shape

Unit 1   Perimeters and areas

Most people know the difference between the perimeter and the area of a shape, but tend to muddle up the formulas used to calculate them. This unit should help you sort out these formulas.

You will also be asked to enter some simple programs on your calculator which will make calculating perimeters and areas a piece of cake!

The *area* is the space inside the shape. Here it is about 8 **square centimetres**.

The *perimeter* is the distance around the outer edge of the shape. Here it is about 12 **centimetres**.

(1)   Where in the world...?

In the world outside the mathematics classroom you will probably need to calculate areas more frequently than perimeters.

Decide whether you would need to know the perimeter or the area of the shape in order to answer each of the questions below.

(a) How many fencing panels are needed for my garden?

(b) How much grass seed do I need for the new lawn?

(c) How many paving slabs are needed for the patio?

(d) What length of wallpaper border will I need in the dining room?

(e) How many square metres of carpet are required?

(f) How long will it take to paint the ceiling?

(g) How much wheat can a farmer grow in a field?

(h) How long will it take to walk around a reservoir?

(i) How long will it take to paint the boundary line of a sports field?

(j) How many parking spaces can be created in a new car park?

(2)   Forming formulas

(a) For each of these shapes write down two formulas, one for the perimeter and one for the area.

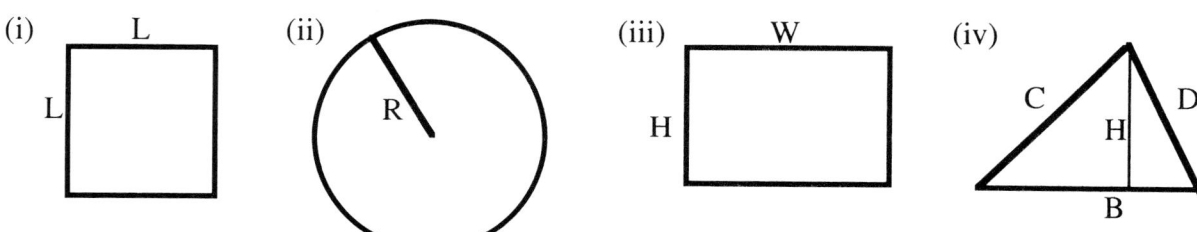

(b) Which of the formulas in part (a) involve adding lengths and which involve multiplying lengths together?

© Alan Graham and Barrie Galpin

Calculator Maths: Shape

(3) Calculator shapes

(a) Execute the program **SETSCRN**.   (i)

Press [2nd] [DRAW] **9** [ENTER] to produce a grid of points. What are the perimeters and areas of the shapes which have been drawn on the screens shown here?

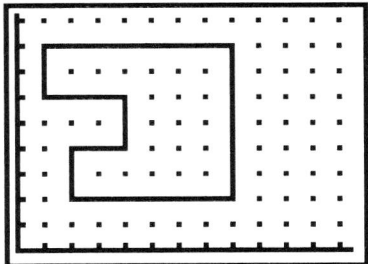

(b) Draw another shape like these which joins the grid points using horizontal and vertical lines.

To do this start on the Graphing screen and:
    press [2nd] [DRAW] **2**,   (ii)
    move to a grid point,
    press [ENTER] to start a line,
    move to the end of the line,
    press [ENTER] [ENTER],
    repeat the last two steps until the shape is finished.

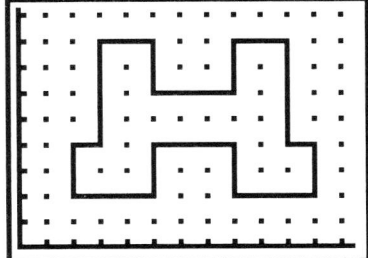

(c) Calculate the perimeter and area of the shape you have drawn. If possible, hand the calculator to someone else to check your calculations.

Brain stretcher   **Internal points**

How many grid points are contained within the boundary of the shapes in Activity 3?

Can you find a relationship between the perimeter, the area, and the number of internal grid points?

Before going any further you should remove the grid points from the Graphing screen by pressing [2nd] [DRAW] **0** [ENTER].

(4) Tree hugging

Three friends find that they can just join hands around the trunk of a large oak tree in the forest.

(a) Estimate the circumference (or perimeter) of the tree trunk.

(b) Use the appropriate formula from Activity 2 to calculate the radius of the tree trunk. What is its approximate diameter?

(c) Use the appropriate formula from Activity 2 to calculate the approximate cross-sectional area of the tree trunk.

© Alan Graham and Barrie Galpin

Calculator Maths: Shape

(5) An extra calculator button

Your calculator cannot work out the area of a circle directly, but by writing a simple program you can give it an 'extra button' to do this.

> The formula for the area of a circle with radius R is
> $A = \pi R^2$.

You could call the program **CIRCLE**. The necessary key presses are given below.

[PRGM] [◄] 1 CIRCLE [ENTER]

[PRGM] [►] 1 [ALPHA] R [ENTER]

[2nd] [π] [ALPHA] R [x^2] [STO►] [ALPHA] A [ENTER]

[PRGM] [►] 2 [ALPHA] A [ENTER]

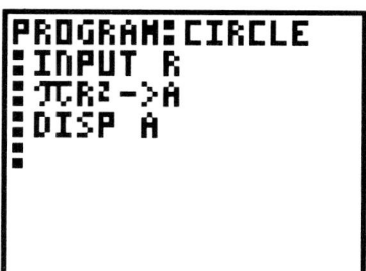

Press [2nd] [QUIT].

Now execute the program by pressing [PRGM] followed by the number or letter of program **CIRCLE** and then [ENTER].

? should appear on the screen, which is asking you to input a radius to store in R. Enter any number you wish. Press [ENTER] and you will see the area of the circle.

To execute the program again you only need to press [ENTER].

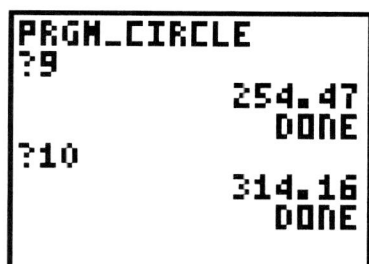

(6) Upgrading your program

(a) You can improve the program by including some text on the screen when the program is executed. You will need to edit the program as follows.

Press [PRGM] [►] and the number of program **CIRCLE**.

Press [►] [2nd] [ALPHA] "RADIUS?" [ALPHA] [,] [ALPHA] R

[▼] [▼]

[2nd] [ALPHA] "AREA [2nd] [TEST] 1 [ALPHA] " [,] [ALPHA] A

Press [2nd] [QUIT] and test the program.

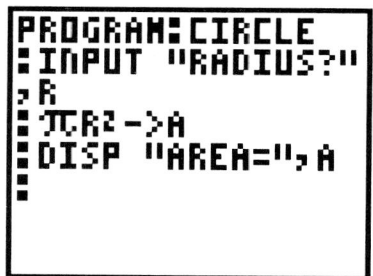

(b) Add two extra commands to your program so that it also calculates and displays the circumference of the circle.

(7) Using the program

Press [MODE] and set your calculator to show two decimal places. Use the program **CIRCLE** to calculate the area of circles which have the following radii:

    (a) 100cm   (b) 7mm   (c) 15.2m.

The program does not produce the units of the answers – don't forget that areas are given in square units.

Calculator Maths: Shape

(8) A piece of cake

A circular birthday cake has a diameter of 30cm and it is cut into 9 equal pieces. Use your calculator where appropriate to answer the following questions. Give your answers correct to the nearest whole number.

(a) What is the radius of the cake?

(b) What is the area of the top of the cake?

(c) What is the area of the top of each piece of cake?

(d) What is the perimeter of the top of each piece of cake?

(9) Yet more buttons

Add some more programs to your calculator which will help you calculate areas and/or perimeters of other simple shapes.

You could try (a) rectangles (see Activity 2),
             (b) triangles (see Activity 2),
             (c) trapeziums (the area a trapezium is the average of the two parallel sides multiplied by the distance between them).

(10) Fenced in

A farmer has a 60m length of electric fencing. She wants to use it alongside a long straight permanent fence to create a rectangular area enclosing as much land as possible. Is this the best arrangement?

Here is a way to investigate this using the calculator's lists.

Clear list L1 and enter lots of possible lengths for the top of the field; try all sorts of numbers between 0 to 60.

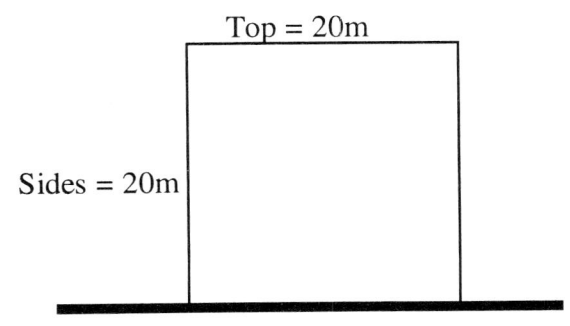

On the Home screen enter **(60−L1)/2−>L2**. This calculates the sides. Why?

On the Home screen enter **L1×L2−>L3**. This calculates the areas. Why?

Which top and sides give the biggest area?

Try the same question with other lengths of electric fencing.

Discussion

- What units are used to measure perimeters and areas?
- The areas of fields are often given in hectares or acres. What are these units?
- Are the perimeter and the area of a shape ever the same?

© Alan Graham and Barrie Galpin

Calculator Maths: Shape

Unit 2 Volumes

Most maths is done on paper.

This can cause problems when dealing with the maths of three dimensional (3-D) shapes like cubes, cylinders, cones and so on. These objects really need to be handled and viewed from different directions if you are to appreciate their properties fully.

If at all possible, try to do this as you work through this unit.

(1) Sugar lumps

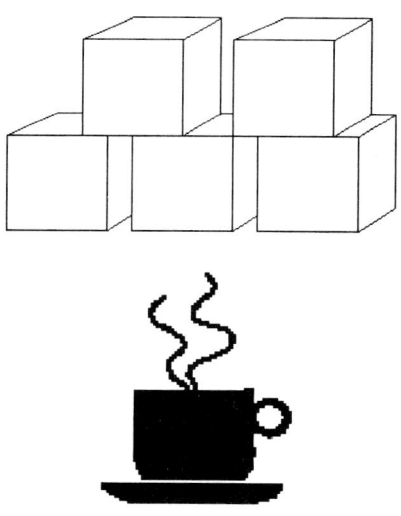

(a) Sugar lumps made by different manufacturers come in various sizes. Assuming the 'lump' is a perfect cube (a big assumption!), calculate the volume of a sugar lump which is 9mm along the side. Include the correct units in your answer.

(b) Write a simple program with the name **CUBEVOL** which lets you input a length of side of a cube and outputs its volume. Use the program to calculate the volumes of each of these cubes with length of side:

   1.2cm, 8mm, 0.6inches.

Include the correct units in your answers.

(c) Alice normally takes three standard-sized sugar lumps with her tea. She buys a new box of smaller cubes with sides exactly half that of her usual ones. How many of the new sugar cubes should she take with her tea?

(2) Shoe box

Capacity means the amount of space inside a container.

(a) A shoe box has internal measurements $35 \times 20 \times 15$cm. Calculate its capacity.

Include the units in your answer.

(b) Give the answer to part (a) in m^3.

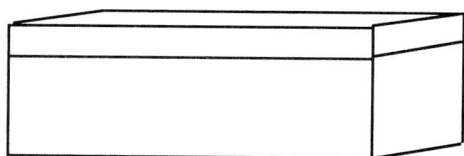

The mathematical name for a shoe box shape is **cuboid**.

10

© *Alan Graham and Barrie Galpin*

Calculator Maths: Shape

(3)   Curious cuboids

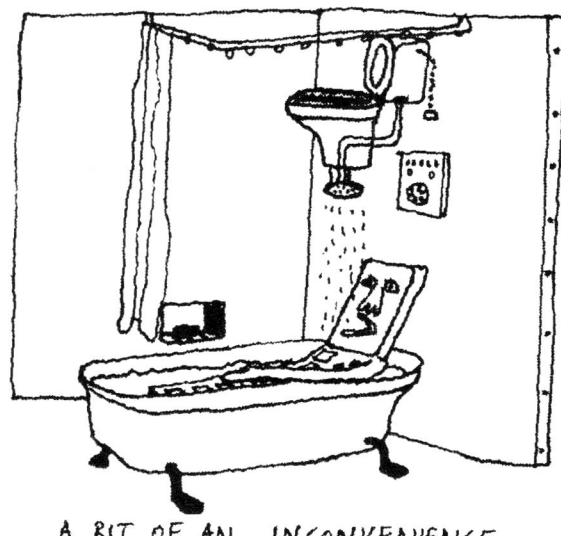

(a) Assume your calculator (with its case) is approximately a cuboid. Measure its dimensions in mm and estimate its volume.

(b) Create a short program called **CUBOID** which lets you input the three sides of a cuboid and outputs the capacity or volume. Use the program to calculate:

- the volume of a brick measuring 22×10×6.5cm,
- the capacity of the room you are sitting in (estimate the dimensions in metres),
- the capacity of the bath in your, or a friend's, bathroom (estimate the dimensions in cm).

(c) A plumber inconveniently re-plumbed the toilet to flush directly into the bath. Assuming the bath plug is left in, estimate how many flushes of the toilet are needed to fill the bath.

A BIT OF AN INCONVENIENCE

(4)   Maxbox

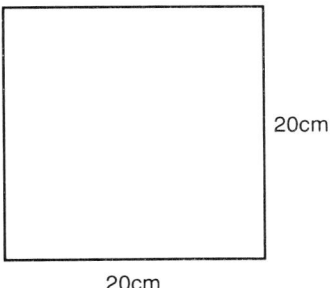   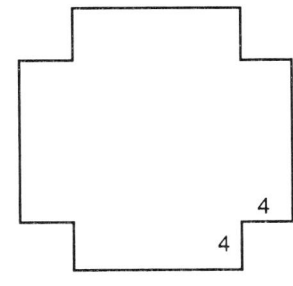   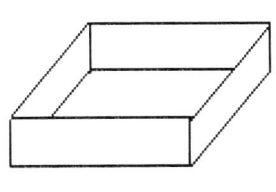

A 20 × 20cm square piece of cardboard ...

... has four identical small squares of side 4cm removed from each corner.

The remaining sides are folded up to make a box (without a lid).

The shape of the box will depend on the size of square cut from the corners and the capacity of the box will vary accordingly. In this activity you can investigate what size of cut-out square produces the largest capacity.

(a) What are the dimensions of this box? Calculate its capacity.

(b) A second 20 × 20cm piece of cardboard has four identical small squares of side 2cm removed from each corner. It is folded to make another box. Calculate the capacity of this box.

(c) Let the length of side of the small squares be *X*. What is the largest value that *X* can take?

(d) Write down a formula for the capacity of the box in terms of *X*.

(e) Press [Y=] and enter the formula from part (d) beside Y1=. Use Table or a graph to investigate what value of *X* produces the box with the largest capacity.

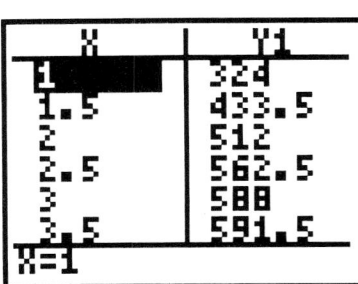

© *Alan Graham and Barrie Galpin*

11

Calculator Maths: Shape

(5) Baked bean tin

The volume of a cylinder, like a baked bean tin, is the area of the circular base times the height.

In Unit 1 you were asked to create a program, **CIRCLE**, which lets you input the radius of a circle and outputs the area. If you haven't already done so, create the program **CIRCLE** now.

Next create a new program to calculate the volume of a cylinder. Press [PRGM] [◄] [ENTER] **CYLINDE** [ENTER].

The first command will be an instruction to carry out program **CIRCLE** in order to calculate the area of the circular base.

Press [PRGM] [◄] and then select **CIRCLE** from the list of programs on your screen. Press [ENTER] to paste **PRGM_CIRCLE** into your program and then press [ENTER] again to move the cursor to the next line.

Complete the program's other commands as shown here.

A can of drink has an approximate diameter of 6cm and an approximate height of 16.5cm. Use **CYLINDE** to check the capacity claimed on the label of 440ml.
How do you account for any discrepancy between the claimed capacity on the label and your answer?

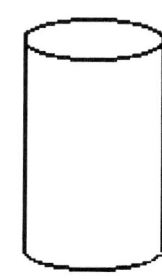

The formula for the volume of a cylinder with radius R and height H is
$$V = \pi R^2 H$$

```
PROGRAM:CYLINDE
:PRGM_CIRCLE
:INPUT "HEIGHT?"
,H
:AH->V
:DISP "VOLUME=",
V
```

(6) On a roll

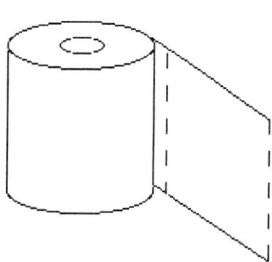

(a) Estimate the outer and inner radius of a new toilet roll. Use the program **CYLINDE** to calculate the approximate volume of paper on the roll.

(b) Estimate the dimensions of a single sheet of toilet paper and calculate its area.

Suppose each sheet were torn off and stacked into a neat pile. Use your answer to part (a) and a suitable calculation to estimate the approximate height of this pile.

(c) Use your answer from part (b) to calculate the approximate thickness of one sheet of paper if there are 280 sheets per roll.

(7) A4

(a) A4 is a standard size of file paper. Find a piece of A4 paper (or another standard size) and measure its length and width accurately in centimetres.

(b) A cylinder can be formed by rolling up the sheet of paper. As shown here, there are two ways of doing this, producing a short, wide cylinder and a tall, thin one.

Guess which of the following is true:
 • the tall, thin cylinder has the larger capacity,
 • the short, wide cylinder has the larger capacity,
 • both cylinders have the same capacity.

(c) Calculate the radius of each cylinder and then use **CYLINDE** to check your guess for part (b).

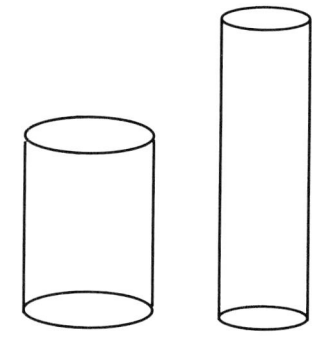

short and wide   tall and thin

The formula for the radius of a circle with cirmference C is
$$R = C/(2\pi).$$

12

© Alan Graham and Barrie Galpin

(8) Wine glass

This conical wine glass has a diameter of 7cm and a depth (to the top of the stem) of 8cm.

(a) Calculate the maximum capacity of the glass.

(b) What proportion of the total capacity of the glass is filled when the wine comes halfway up the glass (i.e. to a depth of 4cm).

(c) To what depth should the glass be filled so that it is half full of wine (i.e. so that there is the same amount of air as wine in the glass)?

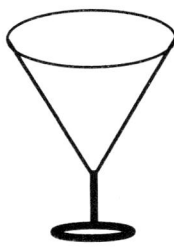

The formula for the volume of a cone with radius R and height H is:
$$V = 1/3\pi R^2 H$$

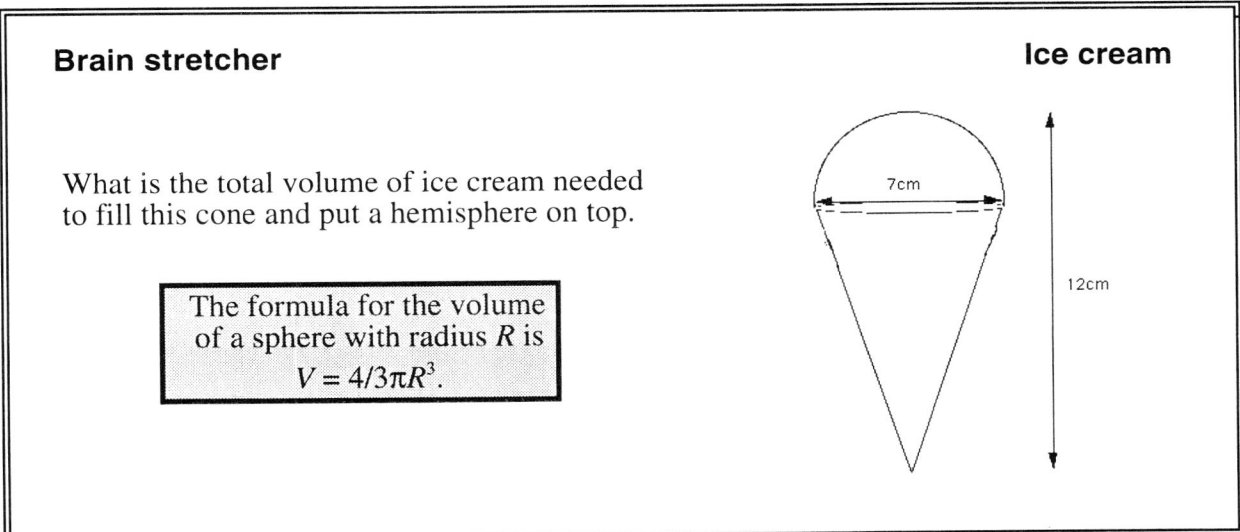

Brain stretcher   **Ice cream**

What is the total volume of ice cream needed to fill this cone and put a hemisphere on top.

The formula for the volume of a sphere with radius R is
$$V = 4/3\pi R^3.$$

Discussion

- Is a cube a cuboid? Is a cuboid a cube?
- What everyday objects have the following shapes: cuboid, cylinder, cone.
- If the length, width and height of a cube are all doubled, what will be the effect on the volume?
- If the length, width and height of any 3-D shape are all doubled, what will be the effect on the volume?
- What is the difference between volume and capacity?
- If you were to draw a series of rectangles all with the same perimeter, the one with the largest area is the square. What is the 3-D version of this result?

© Alan Graham and Barrie Galpin

Calculator Maths: Shape

Unit 3 Pythagoras' theorem

Pythagoras' theorem applies only to **right-angled triangles**.

If you:
- square the lengths of the three sides,
- add the two smaller ones together,
- you get the square of the longest side.

Using symbols: $A^2 + B^2 = C^2$

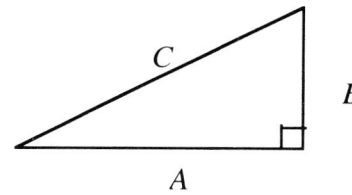

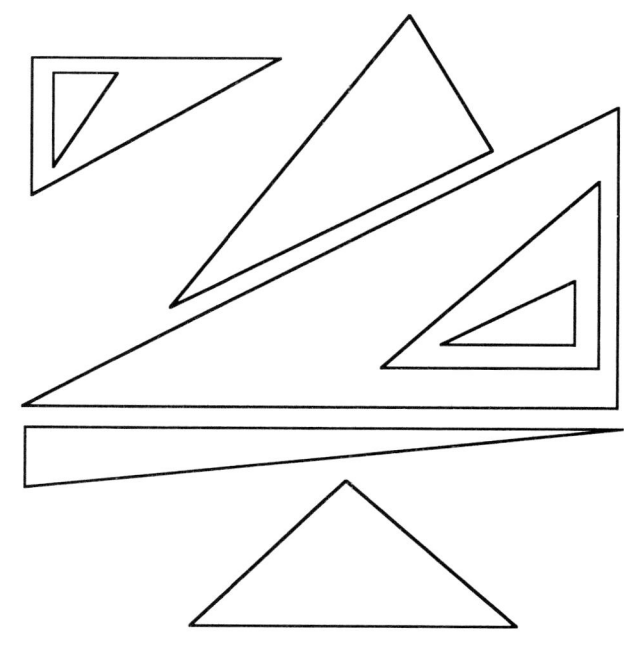

Notice how much easier it is to say it in symbols – and all you have to remember is that *C* stands for the length of the *longest* side.

For example, with a right-angled triangle which has sides of *A*=3, *B*=4 and *C*=5

$$3^2 + 4^2 = 5^2$$

Check: $9 + 16 = 25$

(1) In the playground

A Primary School teacher carefully drew a large triangle in the playground.
She measured the sides and they were 2.1m, 2.8m and 3.5m long.
She wants to be sure that the triangle has a 90° angle.
She enters the following on her calculator.

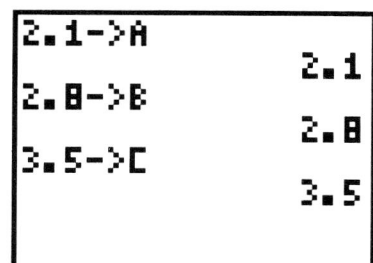
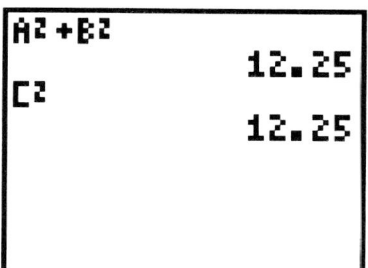

Does the triangle have a 90° angle? Explain carefully why.

(2) It's a right angle, – right?

Another triangle has sides which are 13.2cm, 5.8cm and 14.5cm.
Is it a right-angled triangle?

14   © *Alan Graham and Barrie Galpin*

Calculator Maths: Shape

(3) Whole numbers only

What have these two screen displays to do with Pythagoras' theorem?

```
41²
      1681
9²+40²
      1681
```

```
61²-11²
      3600
60²
      3600
```

(4) Listed measurements

All 9 triangles on the opposite page are right-angled.

Accurately measure the sides of each triangle.

Set the Mode setting to show 1 decimal place.

Enter the measurements in lists L1, L2 and L3. For each triangle:

put the shortest two lengths in L1 and L2;

put the longest length in L3.

Now carry out some list arithmetic (see **Calculator Maths:** *Foundations*, page 40).

Store the result of L1² + L2² in L4.

Store the result of L3² in L5.

Compare the values in L4 and L5. How good were your measurements? Some example measurements are given below. Were yours better than these?

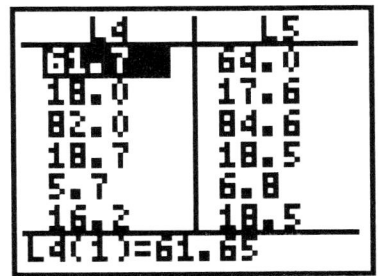

(5) Across the pitch

A football pitch is 100m long and 72m wide.
How far is it between diagonally-opposite corner flags?

Here's one way of calculating this:

- Why is there a square root sign?
- Why are brackets necessary?
- What mode setting has been used?

Now calculate the length of the diagonal of a tennis court which is 36ft wide and 78ft long.

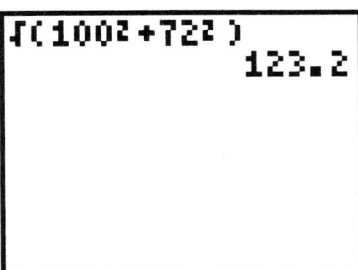

© Alan Graham and Barrie Galpin

Calculator Maths: Shape

(6)   As high as a kite

How high is the kite?

Here is one solution.

$$\sqrt{(60^2 - 39^2)}$$
$$45.59605246$$

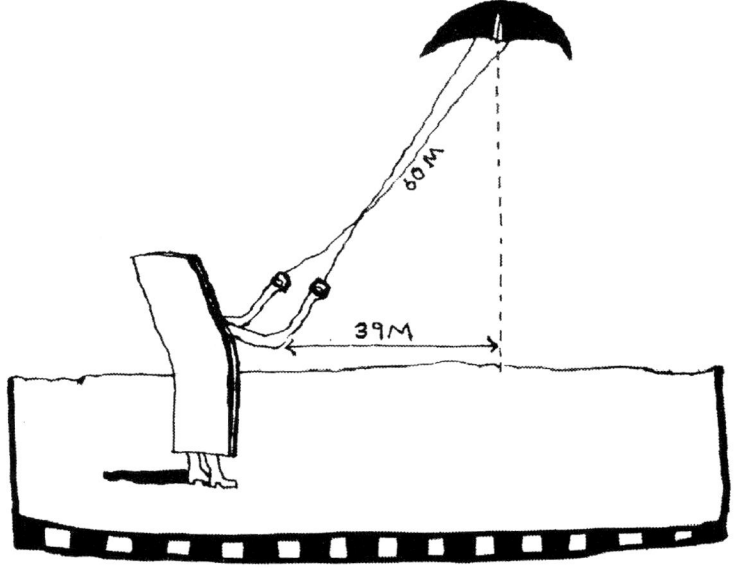

Why is there a *subtract* sign here?

The calculator was set to floating point mode and gave an answer correct to 10 digits. What answer would you give to the question?

Now calculate the height of the kite if the string is 85m and the distance along the ground is 13m.

(7)   Programmed Pythagoras

(a) Here is a program to help you calculate the *longest side* of a right-angled triangle.

Can you explain the third command?

Enter the program and try it out.

(b) Now enter a program called **PYTHAG2** which will help you calculate one of the shorter sides of a right-angled triangle.

Make up some measurements to test your program thoroughly.

(8)   3 – 4 – 5 triangle

(a) The ancient Egyptians and Chinese knew about the special triangle which has sides with lengths

  3 units,
  4 units
  5 units.

Check out this triangle using your calculator.

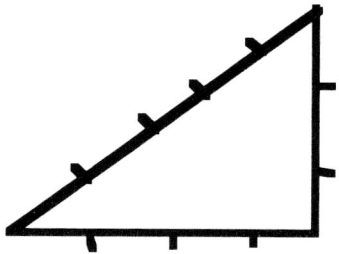

(b) Can you find any other right-angled triangles where the sides are all exact whole numbers? There are some examples in Activities 3 and 6.

  Make a list.
  Look for number patterns.
  Can you predict some more?

Calculator Maths: Shape

(9) Diagonal quiz

This program will test your skills at estimating lengths.

The calculator draws 2 sides of a right-angled triangle. You have to guess the length of the third side.

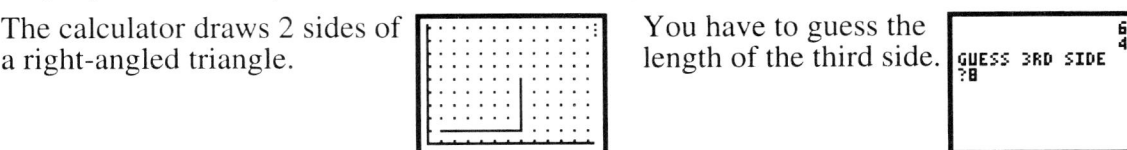

The calculator shows you how good the guess was:

by drawing a line... ...and by doing a calculation.

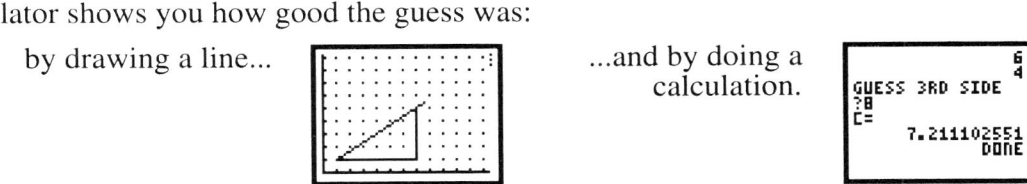

Check that you understand how the program works and enter it on your calculator.

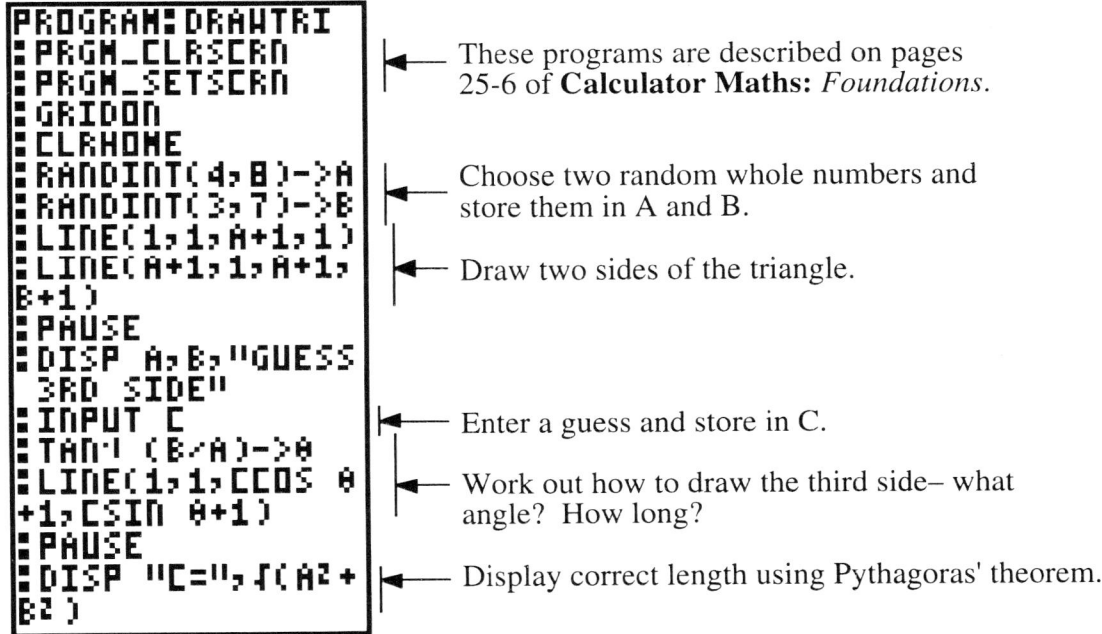

- These programs are described on pages 25-6 of **Calculator Maths:** *Foundations*.
- Choose two random whole numbers and store them in A and B.
- Draw two sides of the triangle.
- Enter a guess and store in C.
- Work out how to draw the third side– what angle? How long?
- Display correct length using Pythagoras' theorem.

Try out your program.

How good are your estimates?

Do you improve with practice?

Discussion

- If you know two sides of a right-angled triangle can you *always* calculate the length of the third side?
- Why are there *two* answers to the question below?
  Two sides of a right angled triangle are 5 units and 12 units.
  What is the third side?
- What effect does the accuracy of measurements have on Pythagoras' theorem?
- When in daily life might you need to use Pythagoras' theorem?

© Alan Graham and Barrie Galpin

Calculator Maths: Shape

Unit 4   Sin, cos and tan

Most people have heard of the 'trig. ratios' sin, cos and tan but what do they really mean?

In this unit, you will investigate what they represent and get practice at using them to calculate the lengths of sides and angles of right-angled triangles.

(1) Triangle

Execute the programs **CLRSCRN** and **SETSCRN**.

Press [2nd] [DRAW] **9** to display a grid of points.

Press [2nd] [DRAW] **2** to select **LINE**.

Move the cursor to position X=2, Y=2 and press [ENTER] to start the line.

Move the cursor to position X=7, Y=2 and press [ENTER] to complete the line.

Press [ENTER] again to start the second line from the same cursor position.

Move the cursor to position X=7, Y=4 and press [ENTER] to complete the second line.

Press [ENTER] again to start the third line from the same cursor position.

Move the cursor back to position X=2, Y=2 and press [ENTER] to complete the third line, as shown here. Look at the vertex of the triangle at (2,2).

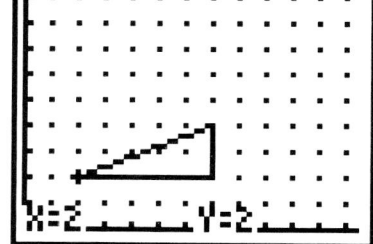

(a) Write down the length of the side *opposite* this vertex (i.e. the vertical side of the triangle).

(b) Write down the length of the side *adjacent* to this vertex (i.e. the horizontal side).

(c) Using Pythagoras Theorem, calculate to 1 d.p. the length of the hypotenuse.

(d) Calculate the following ratios:

(i) $\dfrac{\text{opposite side}}{\text{hypotenuse}}$ (ii) $\dfrac{\text{adjacent side}}{\text{hypotenuse}}$ (iii) $\dfrac{\text{opposite side}}{\text{adjacent side}}$.

(2) Another triangle

Start with its first vertex at (2,5) and draw another triangle with sides exactly twice the length of those of this first triangle.

For the larger triangle, answer parts (a) to (d) as in Activity 1.
Compare your answers to part (d) for the two triangles.
Explain any similarity in the results.

Calculator Maths: Shape

(3) Six similar triangles

(a) Press [2nd] [DRAW] **1** to clear the previous drawings.

Use Option 2, **LINE** from the DRAW menu to draw a triangle with vertices (0,0), (12,0) and (12,8).

(b) Draw five more vertical lines roughly as shown here, making six right-angled triangles in all.

(c) Place the cursor at the right angle of the smallest triangle and make a note of the value of the X coordinate (5.6 in the example shown here).

This is the length of the adjacent side of the smallest triangle. Repeat this process for the other five triangles and enter all six numbers, from smallest to largest, into L1.

(d) Place the cursor at the top vertex of the smallest triangle and make a note of the value of the Y coordinate (3.6 in the example shown here).

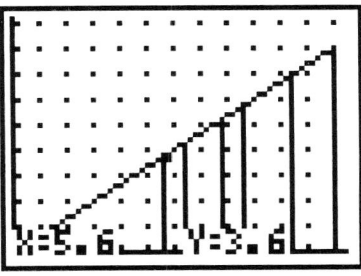

This is the length of the opposite side of the smallest triangle. Repeat this process for the other five triangles and enter all six numbers, from smallest to largest, into L2.

(e) On the Home screen, enter $\sqrt{(L1^2+L2^2)} \rightarrow L3$.

How are the six numbers now stored in L3 linked to the six triangles?

(4) The trig ratios, sin cos and tan

Since the six triangles have the same shape, the ratios of any two sides should be the same for all of them.

Press [MODE].

Fix the calculator display to 2 decimal places by moving the cursor to **2** in the second line and pressing [ENTER].

In the same way choose **DEGREE** in the third line.

Check that your Mode menu appears as shown here.

Return to a clear line on the Home screen.

(a) Enter **L2/L3->L4**.

Look at the six ratios in L4.

All the numbers should be approximately the same. Why is this?

(b) Enter **L1/L3->L5**.

Look at the six ratios in L5.

All the numbers should be approximately the same. Why is this?

(c) Enter **L2/L1->L6**.

Look at the six ratios in L6.

All the numbers should be approximately the same. Why is this?

© Alan Graham and Barrie Galpin

Calculator Maths: Shape

(5) Using [SIN] [COS] and [TAN]

You will need the information in the table here.

Trig ratio	Meaning
sin (short for sine)	$\dfrac{\text{Opposite side}}{\text{Hypotenuse}}$
cos (short for cosine)	$\dfrac{\text{Adjacent side}}{\text{Hypotenuse}}$
tan (short for tangent)	$\dfrac{\text{Opposite side}}{\text{Adjacent side}}$

Measured to the nearest 0.1 degrees, the bottom left angle of the six triangles in Activity 4 is actually 33.7°.

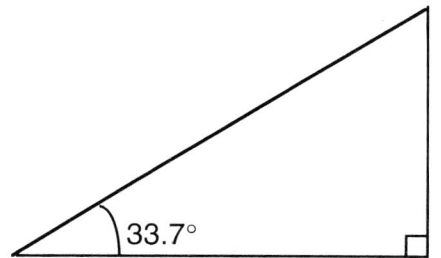

(a) Press [SIN] followed by this number of degrees and then press [ENTER]. Compare your answer with the list of ratios in L4. Can you explain why they are similar?

(b) Repeat part (a), but use [COS] rather than [SIN]. This time compare your answer with the ratios in L5.

(c) Repeat part (a), but use [TAN]. Compare your answer with the ratios in L6.

(6) Calculating trig ratios

(a) Press [MODE] and choose FLOAT.
Press [Y=] and enter the three functions shown here.
Press [2nd] [TBLSET] and enter the settings **TBLMIN=0** and **ΔTBL=15**.
Press [2nd] [TABLE] to see a range of values of sinX. Scroll to the right to see the corresponding values for cosX and tanX.

(b) Using the Table values from part (a), copy and complete the table opposite, giving answers to two decimal places.

(c) What patterns can you see in the numbers in the table in part (b)? Why do you think an ERROR has been produced in one of the columns?

X	sinX	cosX	tanX
0			
15			
30			
45			
60			
75			
90			

(d) You can see from your table that cos 60 = .5. Press [2nd] [COS⁻¹] **.5** [ENTER]. Explain your result.

(e) Press [2nd] [SIN⁻¹] **.2588** [ENTER]. Explain your result.

(f) Press [2nd] [TABLE] and place the cursor on the Y3 value corresponding to 75°. In the table it reads 3.7321, but a more accurate value is given at the bottom of the screen for tan 75°. Write down the value of tan 75° to ten figure accuracy.

With the cursor still positioned on this value of Y3, return to the Home screen and press: [2nd] [TAN⁻¹] [2nd] [Y-VARS] **3** [ENTER]. Explain your result.

Calculator Maths: Shape

Brain stretcher   **Cursor control**

Use the method of Activity 6 to create these screens.

SIN⁻¹ Y1	COS⁻¹ Y2	TAN⁻¹ Y3
60	45	30

(7) Solving triangles

This triangle has side XZ = 6cm and angle X = 25°.

You can calculate the length of the side opposite X, marked O, as follows.

$$\sin 25° = \frac{\text{opposite side}}{\text{hypotenuse}} = \frac{O}{6}.$$

This can be rearranged to read: O = 6 sin 25°.

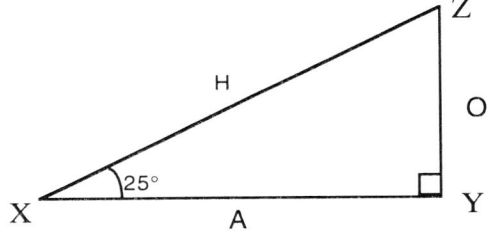

Press **6** [SIN] **25** [STO▶] [ALPHA] **O** [ENTER] to produce the answer 2.54 and store it in location O.

(a) Use a similar method to calculate the length of the side adjacent to angle X, marked A. Store the answer in location A.

(b) Calculate the value of $O^2 + A^2$ and comment on the result.

(c) In the right-angled triangle shown here, the angle at P is 55° and side PR is 12 cm. Calculate the length of the other two sides (accurate to 2 decimal places).

(d) In another right-angled triangle XYZ, the right angle is at Y. The length of side XY = 5.0cm and YZ = 7.0cm, both measurements being accurate to 1 decimal place.

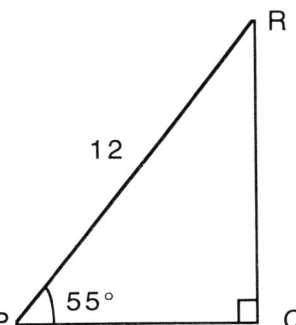

   (i) Use Pythagoras Theorem to calculate the length of XZ, giving your answer to 2 decimal places.

   (ii) Calculate the angles of the triangle.

Discussion

- What do the 2nd functions of the SIN, COS and TAN keys do?
- What are the largest possible values of sinX, cosX and tanX?
- See if you can find a simple formula connecting sinX, cosX and tanX.
- Use TABLE to investigate what happens to trig. ratios for angles greater than 90° and less than 0°.
- Explore the graphs of Y= sinX, Y = cosX, Y= sinX+ 1 and Y= cos(90–X).

© Alan Graham and Barrie Galpin

Calculator Maths: Shape

Unit 5 Similar shapes

The word 'similar' has a different meaning in maths to normal use. You might say, 'Your hairstyle is similar to mine', meaning that, in some vague way, there are certain common features.

In maths, if two shapes are described as 'similar', the features in common are very precisely defined. It means they have *exactly the same shape* but not necessarily the same size. In other words, one is an exact scaled up or scaled down version of the other.

(1) Congruent triangles

Congruent is used to describe two shapes that have exactly the same size and shape. In other words, one is an exact copy of the other.

In this activity you can create a simple shape on the screen (a triangle) and then make exact copies of it.

Store the values {2, 4, 5, 2} in L1 and {1, 2, 6, 1} in L2.

Press [2nd] [STAT PLOT] **1** to select PLOT1. To plot the values in L1 and L2 as a line graph, choose the settings shown here.

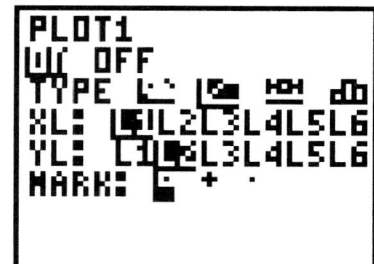

Run the program **SETSCRN** to set a suitable window and see the points joined to make a triangle.

(a) Use TRACE to find the coordinates of the vertices of the triangle.

(b) On the Home screen, add 4 to the values in L1, storing the result in L3. Add 3 to the values in L2, storing the result in L4.

Press [2nd] [STAT PLOT] **2** to select PLOT2. Set STATPLOT to plot the values in L3 and L4 as a line graph and press [GRAPH].

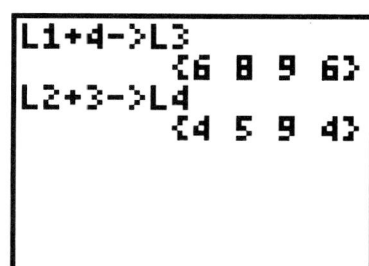

This second triangle is congruent to the first one. What are the coordinates of its vertices?

(c) Use the same method to store suitable values in L5 and L6 and create a third triangle on the screen. Make it congruent to the first two and not overlapping with either of them.

(2) Congruent rectangles

Press [2nd] [STAT PLOT] **4** to select PLOTSOFF.

Clear lists L1 to L6 by pressing:

[STAT] **4** [2nd] [L1] [,] [2nd] [L2] [,] [2nd] [L3] [,] [2nd] [L4] [,] [2nd] [L5] [,] [2nd] [L6] [ENTER]

Enter suitable coordinates into L1 and L2 to draw a small, simple rectangle. Use the method of Activity 1 to create two more non-overlapping congruent rectangles on the screen.

Finally clear the lists once more and press [2nd] [STAT PLOT] **4** to deselect the plots.

© *Alan Graham and Barrie Galpin*

(3) Similar triangles

Similar, as used in maths, describes two shapes that have exactly the same shape but not necessarily the same size. In other words, one is an exact scaled up or scaled down copy of the other.

Store the values {1, 3, 6, 1} in L1 and {2, 4, 3, 2} in L2.

Select PLOT1 and set it to plot the values in L1 and L2 as a line graph. Press GRAPH to see the points joined to make a triangle.

Double the coordinates in L1 and store the result in L3.

Double the coordinates in L2 and store the result in L4.

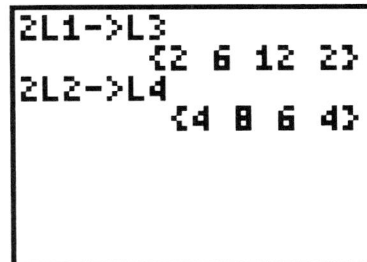

Select PLOT2, switch it back on and press GRAPH.

This second triangle is similar, in the mathematical sense, to the first one (it has the same shape but a different size).

(a) What are the coordinates of the vertices of these two triangles?

(b) Using the method described above, store suitable values in L5 and L6 to create a third triangle on the screen similar to the first two.

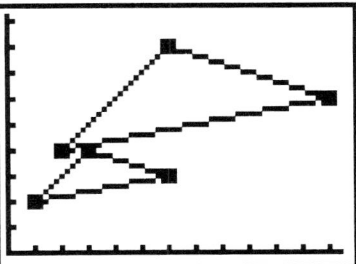

(4) Similar rectangles

Clear lists L1 to L6 and turn the STAT PLOTS off.

(a) Enter suitable coordinates into L1 and L2 to draw this small rectangle.

(b) Use the method of Activity 3 to create the similar rectangle three times as long and three times as high shown here.

Are the two displayed rectangles similar?

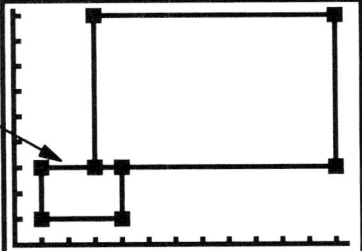

(c) Deselect PLOT2. Using PLOT3, create a third rectangle whose X coordinates are formed by halving the values in L1 and whose Y coordinates are formed by doubling the values in L2.

Are the two displayed rectangles similar?

Clear the lists and turn the STAT PLOTS off.

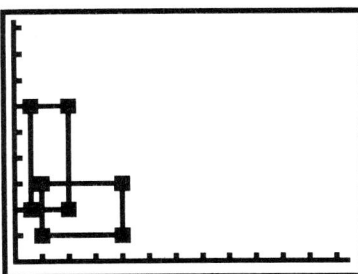

© Alan Graham and Barrie Galpin

Calculator Maths: Shape

(5) Odd rectangle out

(a) Look at these three rectangles. Two are similar to each other and the third one is not.

Which is the odd one out?

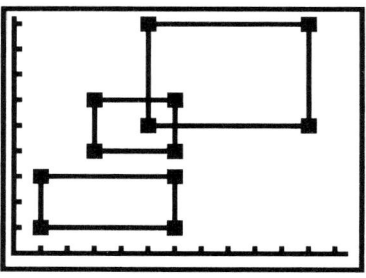

(b) Each pair of lists below produces a rectangle when plotted as a line graph. Two are similar to each other and the other one is not.

Plot these rectangles and decide which is the odd one out?

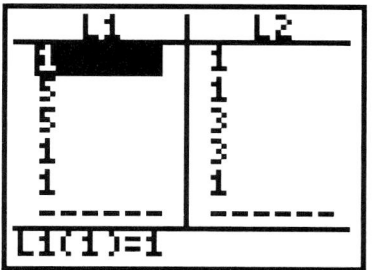 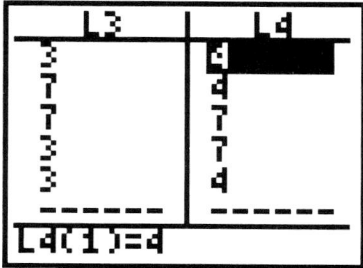 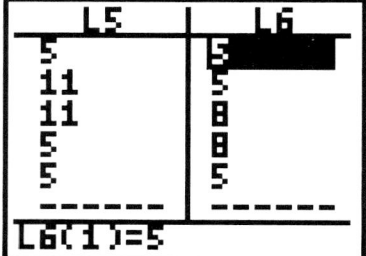

(c) Two rectangles and the corresponding coordinates for their vertices are shown below. Are these rectangles similar?

Why?/why not?

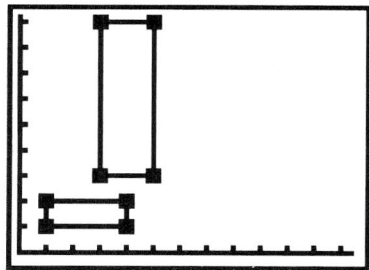 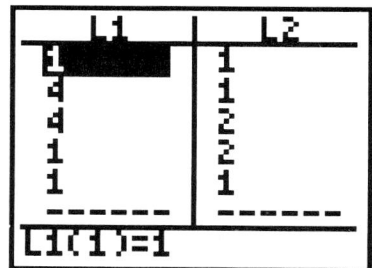 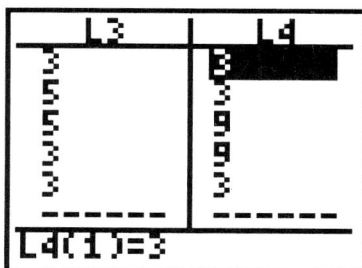

(6) In proportion

When two shapes are similar, the sides are in proportion.

You can check this with the similar triangles which you drew in Activity 3. They are shown again here.

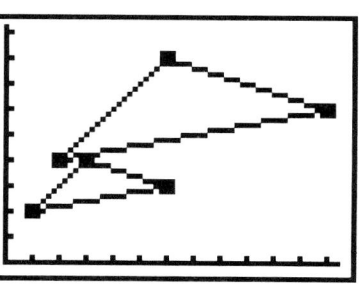

(a) Use a ruler to measure, in millimetres, the three sides of the smaller triangle shown here and enter these numbers into L1. Measure the three sides of the larger triangle in the same order and enter the lengths into L2. Store L2/L1 in L3 and confirm that the numbers in L3 are roughly equal. Explain why.

(b) Clear the statistics lists again. Create two more similar triangles on the screen. As you did with part (a), measure the sides of each triangle, entering the lengths into two lists. Calculate the ratio of these lengths and confirm that they are roughly equal.

Why might the ratios not work out to be *exactly* equal?

Calculator Maths: Shape

> **Brain stretcher**   **Scaling and shifting**
>
> The dimensions of the middle triangle are double those of the inner one and the dimensions of the outer triangle are three times those of the inner one.
>
> Create this screen, or one like it, using as simple a method as possible.

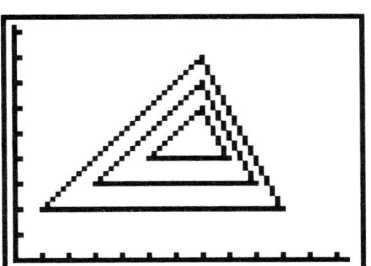

(7) Box of juice

A 1 litre box of juice can be made from the net shown here. The external measurements are 203×93×57mm.

(a) Estimate the capacity of the box based on these external measurements.

(b) Calculate the percentage by which this capacity exceeds the stated capacity of 1 litre.

How do you account for the difference between the stated capacity and your answer to part (a)?

(c) If all the dimensions of the box are reduced by 10%, by what percentage will the capacity be reduced?

(d) A half litre box is the same shape as this litre box. How tall is it?

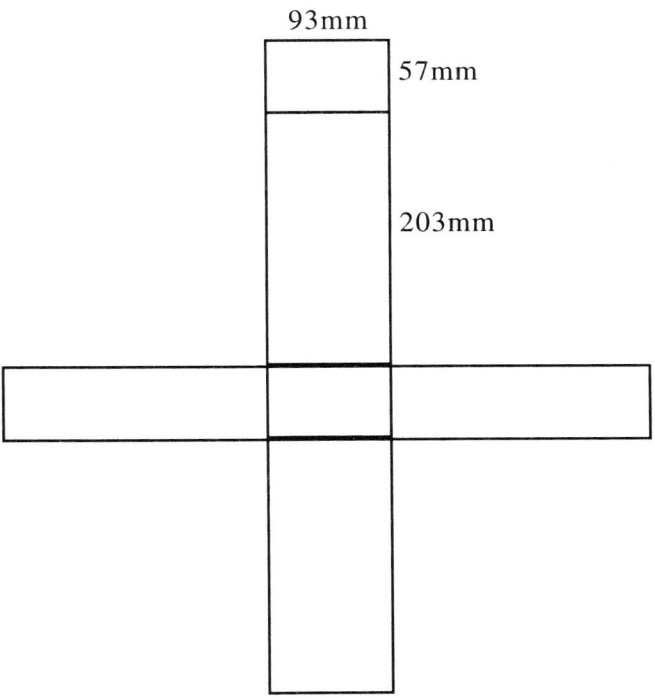

Discussion

- Are all rectangles similar? What about squares, circles, triangles, equilateral triangles, right-angled triangles...?
- If two triangles are similar, what can you say about their angles?
- If two rectangles are similar, what can you say about the lengths of their sides?
- If two shapes are similar, are they necessarily congruent?
- If two shapes are congruent, are they necessarily similar?
- If the dimensions of a 2-D shape are doubled, what happens to the area?
- If all the dimensions of a 3-D shape are doubled, what happens to the volume?
- Can you think of three ways of altering a shape?

© Alan Graham and Barrie Galpin

Calculator Maths: Shape

Unit 6 Locus

Imagine that you are giving directions to guide a white-line road marker. Think about what sort of instructions would be needed for it to draw, say, a circle or to take some other chosen path.

In mathematics, the instruction, or rule needed to trace a path which produced a shape is called the **locus** of the shape.

(1) A straight line locus

There are various ways of writing a rule to define a locus.
One simple way is to use a rule that connects the *X* and *Y* coordinates.

(a) Explore the locus: 'each *Y* coordinate equals twice its *X* coordinate', as follows:

Enter a SEQ command to store the whole numbers from -5 to 5 in L1. These are the *X* coordinates.

Store twice the numbers in L1 into L2.

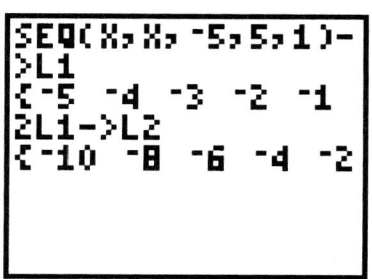

Press [2nd] [STAT PLOT] and choose the settings to plot the values in L1 and L2 as a scatterplot.

Press [ZOOM] **6** to select a suitable window and press [TRACE].

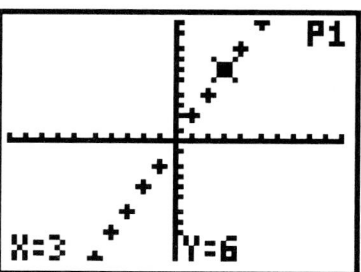

Repeatedly press [▶]. As you do so, confirm for each pair of coordinates that the locus rule is correct.

(b) The rule applies not just to the whole numbers plotted here but also to all the possible points in between.

You can see this by graphing the line *Y*=2*X*.

Press [Y=] and enter **Y1=2X**. Press [TRACE] [▼].

Scroll along the line using [▶] and [◀].
What values of Y on this line correspond to the following X values?

   X=3.2258,   X=6.129,   X=-2.258.

(c) Press [2nd] [STAT PLOT] **4** to select PLOTSOFF.

Place the cursor at the origin and press [ZOOM] **2** [ENTER].
When the new line is drawn, press [ENTER] again.
Continue to press [ENTER] three more times.
Press [TRACE] and scroll along the line using [▶] and [◀].

What values of Y on this line correspond to the following X values?

   X=.01008,   X=.12097,   X=⁻.0605.

Finally, press [Y=] and clear the equation **Y1=2X**.

Calculator Maths: Shape

(2) Another straight line locus

(a) Here is a second locus:
'each Y coordinate equals 5 more than its X coordinate'.

Store the whole numbers from −10 to 5 in L1 as the X coordinates. To create this locus, store suitable Y coordinates in L2. Press [TRACE], repeatedly press ▶ and ◀ and check the coordinates displayed on the screen to confirm that you have entered the new locus rule correctly.

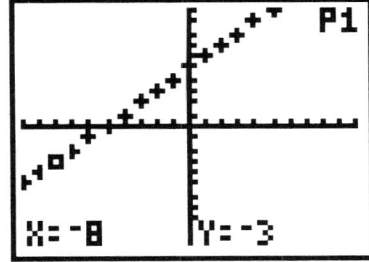

(b) Press [Y=] and enter alongside Y1= a suitable straight line equation which will pass through the points.

(c) Select PLOTSOFF to deselect the scatterplot.
Press [TRACE].
What are the coordinates of where this line cuts the two axes?

(d) Zoom in repeatedly on the point where the line cuts the Y axis. Use Table to find the values of Y on this line corresponding to the following X values?
    X = .00158,   X = 6.3E-4,   X = −9E-6.

(3) A plague of locuses

Below are eight locus descriptions and eight pictures (all drawn using the setting Zoom Standard) but they are not matched up. Match each locus to its picture and write down the corresponding equation for each locus.

PSST. ACTUALLY, THE PLURAL OF 'LOCUS' IS 'LOCI'

(a) 'Each Y coordinate equals five less than three times its X coordinate.'

(b) 'Each Y coordinate equals three times the value that is five less than its X coordinate'

(c) 'Each Y coordinate equals four less than the square of its X coordinate.'

(d) 'Each Y coordinate equals the square of the value that is four less than its X coordinate.'

(e) 'Each Y coordinate equals one divided by its X coordinate.'

(f) 'Each Y coordinate equals six.'

(g) 'Each Y coordinate equals zero.'

(h) 'Each X coordinate equals minus three.'

(i)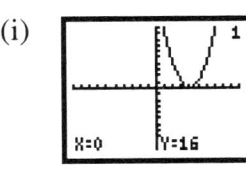

(iii)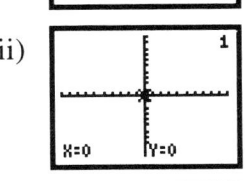

(v)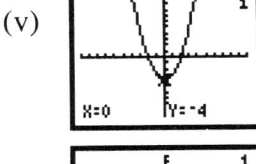

(vii)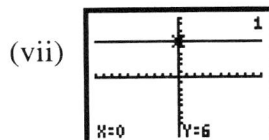

(ii)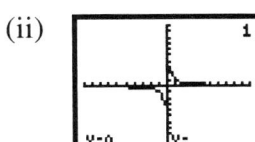

(iv)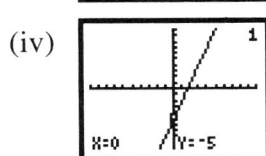

(vi)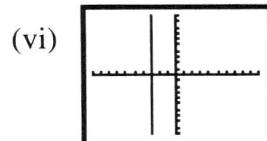

(viii)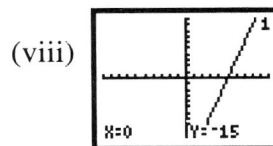

© Alan Graham and Barrie Galpin

Calculator Maths: Shape

(4) Painting the road

Run **CLRSCRN** to clear all existing Y= graphs.
Run **SETSCRN** to select a convenient graphing screen.

(a) From the Graphing screen, press [2nd] [DRAW] **3** to select a horizontal line. Hold down [▲] until the Y coordinate reads **Y=6** and then press [ENTER] to fix the line.

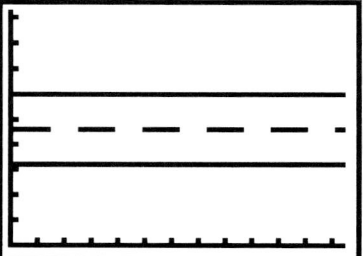

Hold down [▼] until the Y coordinate reads **Y=3.2** and again press [ENTER] to fix the line. A 'road' now runs across the screen.

Press [2nd] [DRAW] **2** and draw a series of short lines in the middle of the 'road'.

Describe in mathematical terms the locus of this dashed line in relation to the two horizontal lines.

(b) Press [2nd] [DRAW] **1** to clear the drawings.

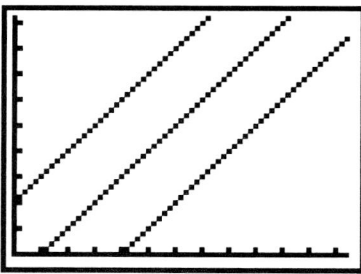

Now draw **X=3** and **X=7.4** to represent a vertical road and draw a continuous line down the middle.

(c) The three lines shown here were drawn from the Y= screen. Create this picture or one similar to it.

(d) Make the road run from top left to bottom right with a line down the centre.

(5) Equidistant from two other points

This program lets you investigate the locus of points which are the same distance from two fixed points, (A,B) and (C,D).

First execute program **SETSCRN** to set a suitable window and set up STATPLOT to produce a scatterplot of L1 against L2.

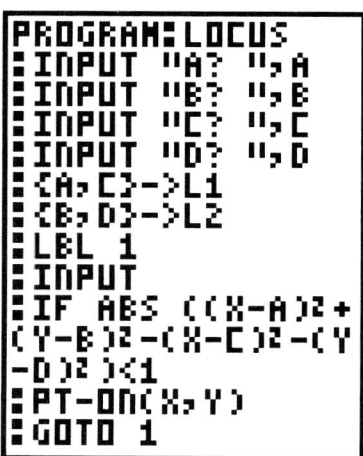

Now enter the program **LOCUS** shown here.

When the program is run you will be asked to input the coordinates of the two fixed points and these will be plotted on the Graphing screen.

Now you must try to decide which points on the Graphing screen are an equal distance from your two fixed points. Use the cursor keys to move to any point you think lies on this locus. Press [ENTER] and, if you are right, a dot appears on the screen.

Try lots of points until the locus appears clearly.

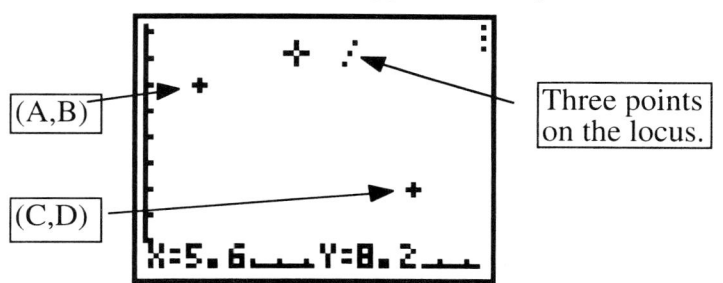

When you have finished plotting the locus press [ON] to quit from the program.

28 © Alan Graham and Barrie Galpin

(6) Tethered goat

(a) A goat is tethered to a post in a field. What is the locus of the biggest path it can walk (when the rope is tightly stretched)?

(b) Plot the goat's path as follows:

Press [ZOOM] **6** to select the standard window settings. Assume that the rope is 8 metres long and the post here is at the **origin**.

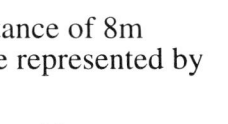

The locus of the goat's path is a fixed distance of 8m from the origin. Let the goat's position be represented by coordinates (X,Y).

Using Pythagoras' Theorem: $X^2 + Y^2 = 8^2 = 64$.

Rearranging $\qquad Y^2 = 64 - X^2$

Taking the square root, $\qquad Y = \sqrt{(64 - X^2)}$

Press [Y=] and enter **Y1 = √(64 − X²)**. Press [GRAPH].

(c) Oops! Not much of a circle! There are two problems here:

- The bottom half of the circle is missing – because the calculator gives only the positive square root and so the negative part of the curve is ignored.

- The circle looks squashed – because the screen is not square.

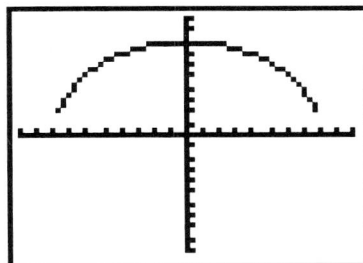

Solve these problems as follows:

To create the negative part of the curve, place the cursor to the right of Y2= and press: [(-)] [2nd] [Y-VARS] **1**

To 'square up' the graph, select ZSQUARE by pressing [ZOOM] **5**.

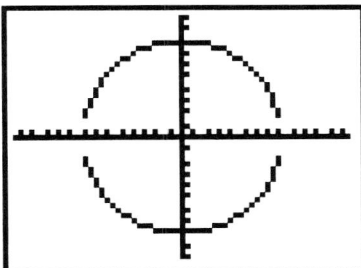

Brain stretcher   **Cross**

Run program **SETSCRN** to produce a suitable screen with 'square' axes.
Draw one vertical and one horizontal line which intersect at (6,5).
(a) What is the locus of a line equidistant from these two lines?
(b) Graph this third line by entering its equation(s) in the Y= screen.

Discussion

- How could you mark out a circular flower bed using string and two poles?
- How could you mark out an elliptical flower bed using string and three poles?

Calculator Maths: Shape

Unit 7 Polygons

In this unit you will use your calculator to draw polygons in various ways.

The word 'polygon' comes from two Greek words; *poly* meaning *many* and *gon* meaning *knee* (or corner).

Shapes with three or four corners and sides are polygons too, even though three or four does not really seem very many. So triangles, squares and other quadrilaterals will appear in this unit.

Any **regular** polygon has all its sides the same length and all its angles equal.

You will need to use the **DEGREE** setting in the Mode menu, so if necessary change this now.

(1) A regular pentagon

Pentagons have five sides.

Here is one way of drawing a regular pentagon on paper.

- Draw a circle and mark its centre.
- Measure angles of 360° ÷ 5 = 72° at the centre and draw 5 equally spaced radii.
- Join up the points where the radii meet the circle.

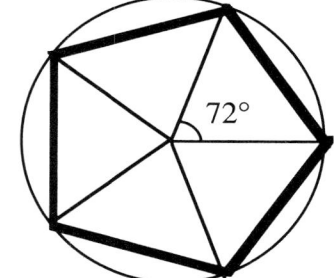

Here is a way of drawing a regular pentagon on your calculator.

- Press [ZOOM]. Choose **ZDECIMAL** and assume that the centre will be at the origin on the Graphing screen.
- Calculate the *X* coordinates of the five corners and store them in L1 by entering
  SEQ(2COS X,X,0,360,72) –>L1
- Calculate the Y coordinates of the five corners and store them in L2. This is best done by pressing [2nd] [ENTRY] and editing the previous entry so that it reads
  SEQ(2SIN X,X,0,360,72) –>L2
- Press [2nd] [STAT PLOT] and set up PLOT1 to draw a line graph of L1 values against L2 values.

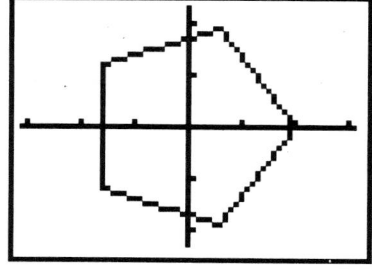

Draw these two pentagons, one on paper and the other on your calculator screen.

What do the two methods have in common?

30 © *Alan Graham and Barrie Galpin*

Calculator Maths: Shape

(2)   Regular polygons

(a)   In Activity 1 you used an angle of 72° to produce a regular 5-sided shape.

Suppose you used 90° instead. What shape would you expect?

Edit the two entries you used in Activity 1, changing the 72 to 90.

Press [GRAPH].

Did you expect it to look like this?

(b)   By editing the entries, try to produce these displays.
What are these shapes called?

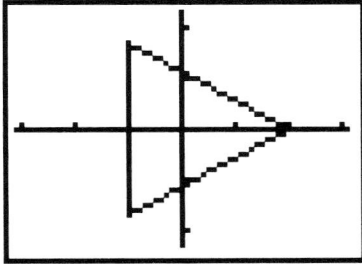 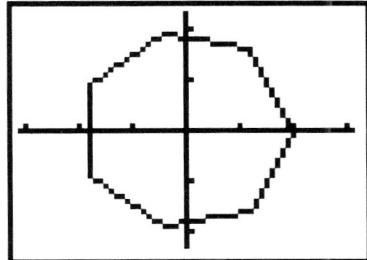

(c)   Calculate the angles you would need to produce a regular hexagon (6 sides), a regular octagon (8 sides) and a regular dodecagon (12 sides).
Make the changes and draw the polygons.

(3)   Polygons or not?

How many sides would you expect if you changed the angles to the following? Imagine what the shape will look like on the calculator and then check your prediction.

   (a)   4°   (b)   180°   (c)   100°

In part (b) you may need to press [TRACE] to find the shape on the Graphing screen.

(4)   Seeing stars

With slight changes in the commands used to store coordinates in L1 and L2 you can produce drawings like those shown below. For example, try entering:

   SEQ(2COS X,X,0,3600,80) ->L1

   SEQ(2SIN X,X,0,3600,80) ->L2

Experiment by changing the 80 to other values.

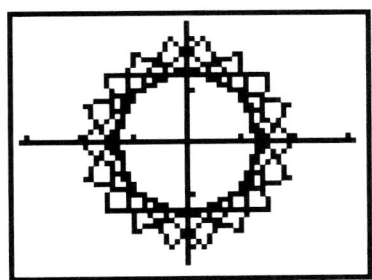 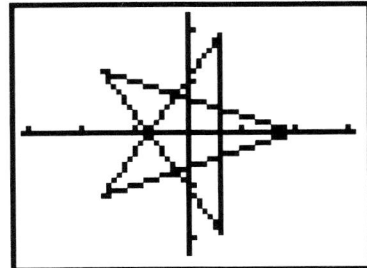 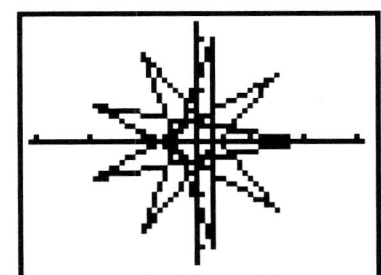

© Alan Graham and Barrie Galpin

Calculator Maths: Shape

(5) Unit squares

Could you write a program to help you draw squares with sides one unit long, starting anywhere on the Graphing screen? If your starting point has coordinates (X,Y) the coordinates of the other 3 corners would be as shown here. Do you agree?

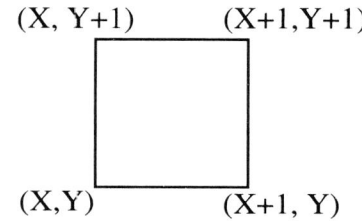

(a) Press [PRGM] [◄] [ENTER] and enter the name of the program **UNITSQS**.

(b) Press [PRGM] [▶] **1** to enter the command **INPUT**.

Usually INPUT must be followed by a store location such as A, but here it is being used in a different way as you will see. Press [ENTER].

(c) Enter **LINE(X,Y,X+1,Y)**, a command to join two of the points. **LINE** is option 2 in the Draw menu.

(d) Enter appropriate **LINE** commands to draw the other three sides of the square.

(e) Press [2nd] [QUIT] and test the program so far.
When the calculator pauses it has reached the INPUT command: move the cursor on the graphing screen to any starting point. When you press [ENTER] the coordinates will be stored in X and Y and the rest of the program will be executed.

(f) Finally add commands to make the program loop back to the first command. To do this add a last command, **GOTO 1,** (use option 8 in the PRGM CTL menu). Then go back to the first command of the program and insert a label there by pressing   [2nd] [INS] [PRGM] **7 1** [ENTER].

(g) Press [2nd] [QUIT] and test the completed program.
When you want to stop drawing squares, press [ON] to interrupt the program.

(6) Polyominoes

In this activity you will investigate the shapes that can be made by placing identical squares side by side (not just corner to corner). Such shapes are sometimes called polyominoes.

Start by executing program **SETSCRN** and add a grid of points by using option 9 of the DRAW menu.

(a) Use the program **UNITSQS** to produce shapes like these, made up of four unit squares placed side to side. They are called tetrominoes.

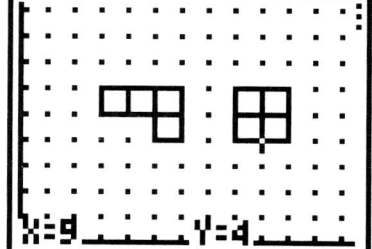

How many different tetrominoes can you find?

(b) Pentominoes are made up of five unit squares.

How many can you find? How many sides does each pentomino have? What sort of polygons are these?

(c) How many different polyominoes are there made up of:

    (i)   3 unit squares (triominoes);

    (ii)   2 unit squares (dominoes);

    (iii)   1 unit square (monominoes)?

Calculator Maths: Shape

(7) Octagons

(a) Write a program similar to **UNITSQS** which will draw octagons in a similar way.
This can be done with eight LINE commands joining points with coordinates as shown here.

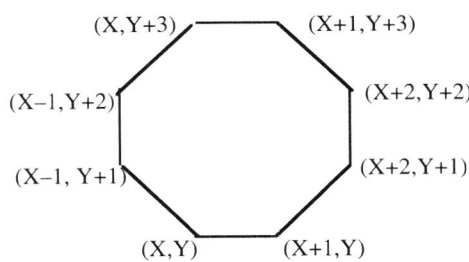

(b) Does the program draw **regular** octagons?

(c) Use the program to produce these **tessellation patterns** made of octagons and squares.

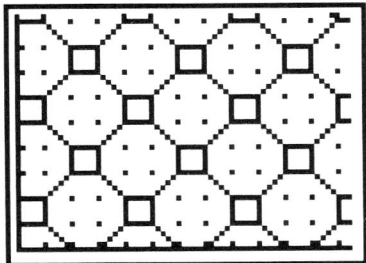
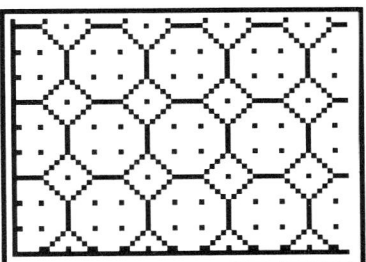

Brain stretcher   **Tessellations**

Write a program which will draw a series of simple shapes.
Using the program, create some tessellations like the ones shown here.

Discussion

- A nonagon is a nine-sided polygon. What names are given to other polygons?
- How would you calculate the size of the angles in regular polygons?
- Is a circle a regular polygon?
- Are polyominoes polygons?

© Alan Graham and Barrie Galpin

Calculator Maths: Shape

Unit 8 Circles

In this unit you will use your calculator in two different ways to draw circles. In order to do this you need to think carefully about what a circle actually *is*.

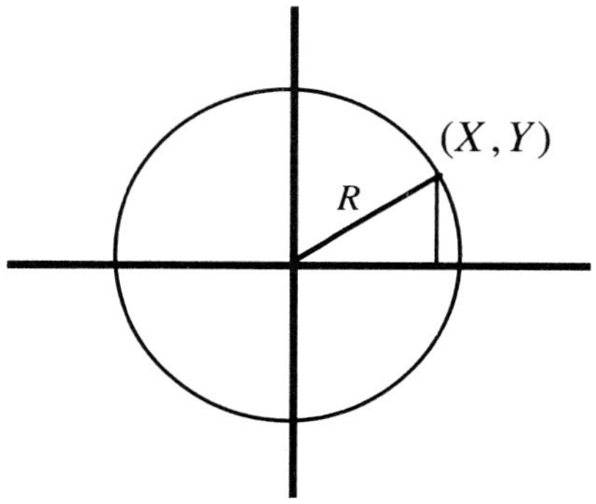

One way of defining a circle is:

the set of points which are the same distance from the centre point.

The diagram on the right shows the set of points which are R units from the centre. R is the **radius** of the circle.

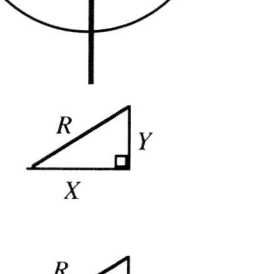

For any point on the circle such as (X,Y), Pythagoras' Theorem says that:

$$X^2 + Y^2 = R^2 \qquad (1)$$

Alternatively if the point (X,Y) makes an angle T with the horizontal at the centre of the circle then using trigonometry:

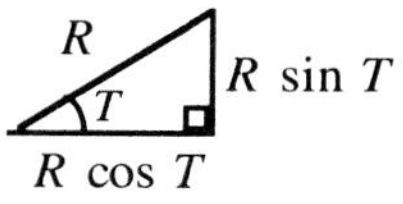

$$X = R \cos T, \quad Y = R \sin T \qquad (2)$$

So equations (1) and (2) provide two alternative descriptions of the circle and both may be used on your calculator.

(1)   Using $X^2 + Y^2 = R^2$

To draw a circle using formula (1) it is necessary to rearrange it to the form $Y = $ something. There are two steps in this process.

$$\text{Take } X^2 \text{ from both sides} \qquad Y^2 = R^2 - X^2$$
$$\text{Take square roots of both sides} \qquad Y = \sqrt{(R^2 - X^2)}$$

(a) Enter this as Y1 by pressing

[Y=] [CLEAR] [2nd] [√] [(] [ALPHA] **R** [x^2] [−] [X,T] [x^2] [)]

On the Home screen store the value 2 in R.

Set a suitable viewing window by selecting option 4, ZDECIMAL from the Zoom menu.

What is drawn on the Graphing screen?

(b) The disappointing result is caused by the square root function. Whereas there should be two values of a square root, one positive and one negative, the calculator can produce only a positive one. (See **Calculator Maths:** *Number*, Unit 2, Squares and square roots, for more details). The negative values of the square root can be produced by entering **Y2 = ⁻Y1**,

To do this press [Y=] [▼] [CLEAR] [(−)] [2nd] [Y-VARS] **1**

Press [GRAPH] to see the completed circle.

(c) By storing different values in R, try drawing circles with different radii.

Calculator Maths: Shape

(2) Tracing the circle

Draw a circle with radius 2 units using the method described in Activity 1.

(a) Press [TRACE] and move to any point on the circle. Notice the values of the *X* and *Y* coordinates displayed at the bottom of the screen.
Move to the Home screen and enter $X^2 + Y^2$. What value is produced?

(b) Press [TRACE] again and try moving to another point, perhaps on the other half of the circle. (To jump to the other half press [▼].)
Move to the Home screen and press [ENTER] to repeat the calculation of $X^2 + Y^2$.

Repeat the procedure for other points on the circle. Can you explain these results?

Brain stretcher   **Bull's-eye**

Can you produce a display similar to the one shown here?

You may find it useful to use option 5 in the Draw menu, DRAWF.

Could you create it with a program?

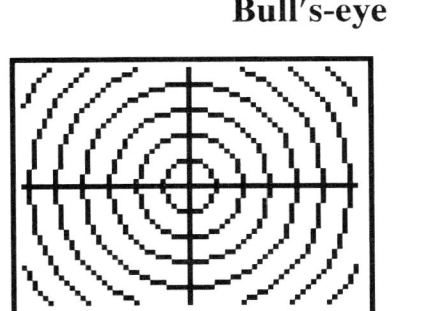

---

3) Using *X* = *R* cos *T*, *Y* = *R* sin *T*

(a) Start by pressing [MODE] and choose the options marked here.

In particular make sure that you have chosen DEGREE and also PARAM, standing for **parametric graphing**. This option makes your calculator draw graphs in a very different way from the normal FUNC or **function graphing**.

(b) Press [ZOOM] 4 [WINDOW]

In parametric graphing you need to set up values of a parameter T. In this case T will stand for the angle at the centre of the circle and it will run from 0 to 360 degrees in steps of 5 degrees.

Make any necessary changes to create these window settings.

(c) Press [Y=] and enter the equations for X1T and Y1T as shown below.

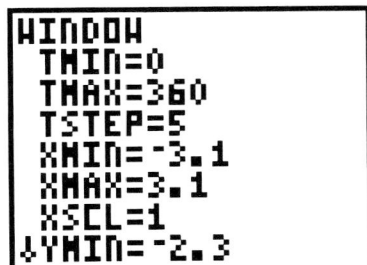
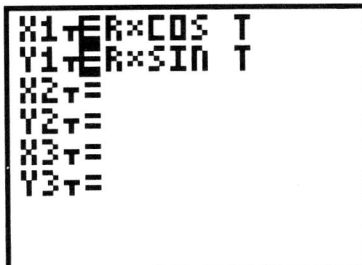

(d) Press [GRAPH].
How is this circle drawn differently from those you produced in Activity 1?

© Alan Graham and Barrie Galpin

Calculator Maths: Shape

(4) Retracing the circle

Draw a circle with radius 2 units using the method described in Activity 3.

Press [TRACE] and move to any point on the circle. Notice that the current value of T as well as the X and Y coordinates is displayed.

Move to the Home screen and enter $X^2 + Y^2$. Notice that when you are in Parametric mode, pressing the [X,T] key produces a T. To enter X you need to press [ALPHA] X.

What value is produced for $X^2 + Y^2$?

On the Graphing screen trace other points on the circle and repeat the calculation of $X^2 + Y^2$. Is this the result you expected?

(5) Two eyes, a nose and ...?

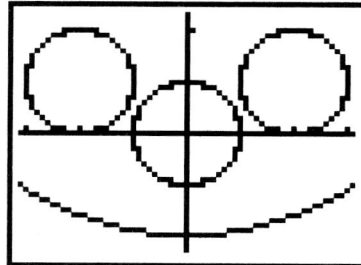

When your calculator is in Parametric mode it is easy to move circles to other positions. To produce the face shown here you need to press the keys listed below.

After each key sequence ask yourself *why* it works.

First check that the Mode menu, window settings and the Y= screen are as shown in Activity 3.

(a) To draw the nose press

[2nd] [QUIT] 1 [STO▶] [ALPHA] R [ENTER] [GRAPH]   (*Why?*)

(b) To draw the right eye press

[Y=] [▼] [▼] [2nd] [Y-VARS] [▶] 1 [+] 2 [ENTER]
[2nd] [Y-VARS] [▶] 2 [+] 1 [GRAPH]   (*Why?*)

(c) To draw the left eye...well, over to you!

(d) To draw the mouth press

[2nd] [DRAW] 5 0.1 [ALPHA] X [x²] [−] 2 [ENTER]

(e) Try the effect of storing different values in R, changing the equations on the Y= screen and drawing different functions.

(6) Wheels

Use a method similar to that of Activity 5 to draw circles representing the wheels of a vehicle. The rest of the vehicle can be drawn using option 2 of the Draw menu.

Calculator Maths: Shape

(7) Round the circle

For this activity you will need a selection of circular objects such as tins, cups, vases, saucepans, cake tins etc. You will also need a tape measure or piece of string and a ruler.

(a) Find as many circular objects as you can and very carefully measure the **circumference** (that is the distance round the circle) and the **diameter** (that is the distance straight across through the circle's centre). Record your measurements in centimetres, correct to 1 decimal place.

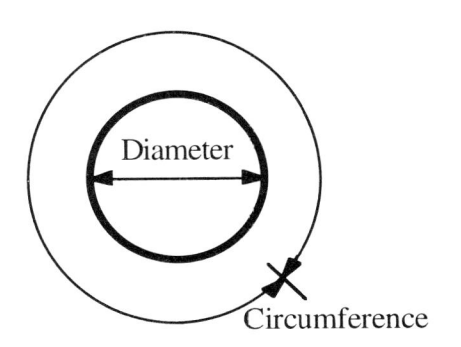

(b) Clear lists L1, L2 and L3.

Enter the diameters in list L1 and the corresponding circumferences in list L2.

The screen shown here gives the measurements recorded for a baked bean tin, a tin of tuna, a tea caddy, a saucepan and two different cake tins. If you are unable to measure any objects yourself you could use these values instead.

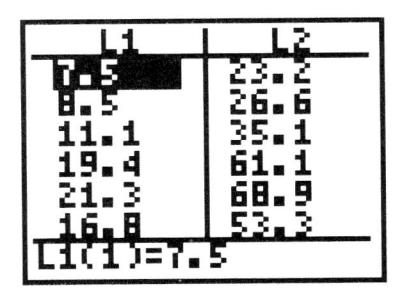

(c) On the Home screen enter **L2/L1->L3**.

What do you notice about the values in L3?

(d) Use 1-VAR STATS to calculate the mean of the values in L3.

(e) Set up a statistical plot to show a scatterplot of the values in L1 plotted against those in L2. Choose a suitable viewing window and produce the scatterplot. Do the points seem to lie on a straight line? Remember the X coordinates represent diameters and the Y coordinates represent the circumferences of circles.

(f) On the Y= screen enter **Y1=π X**. [π] is the second function of the [^] key.

Press [GRAPH]. How well does this line fit the points of the scatterplot?

(g) On the Home screen press [2nd] [π] [ENTER] to see the value of π. How does this compare with your answer to (d), the mean of the circumferences divided by the diameters?

(h) What does all this tell you about the relationship between the circumference and the diameter of circles? Can you express this as a formula?

(i) What is the relationship between the circumference and the radius of circles?

Discussion

- What is a circle? Is it just the points on a line or the points inside it too?
- Which of the two methods of drawing a circle on your calculator do you prefer and why?
- What is this number π?
- The radius of a circle is doubled. What happens to its area and its circumference?

© Alan Graham and Barrie Galpin

Calculator Maths: Shape

Unit 9 Transforming shapes

Look carefully at this screen display.

A basic **object** has been transformed into two different **images**. You can tell which are which by looking at the corners of the shapes. In this unit images have crosses or boxes at their corners.

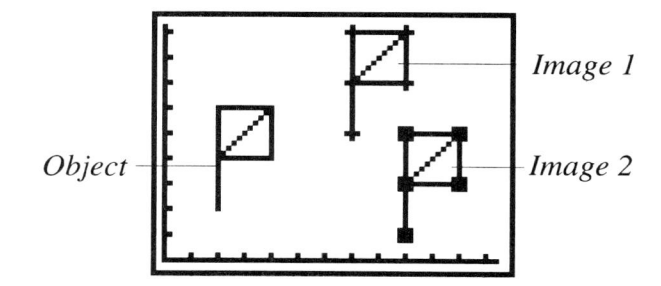

The coordinates of the corners of the object have been stored in lists L1 and L2. Some arithmetic has been carried out on L1 and L2 to produce values which have been stored in L3 and L4. The same process has been repeated for L5 and L6.

Each shape has been produced using a separate line graph. PLOT1 joins the values in L1 and L2 (the object), PLOT2 the values in L3 and L4 (Image 1), and PLOT3 the values in L5 and L6 (Image 2).

What types of transformation are shown here and what arithmetic has been carried out to produce them? Work through the activities in this unit and you will be able to answer these questions and create similar screen displays yourself.

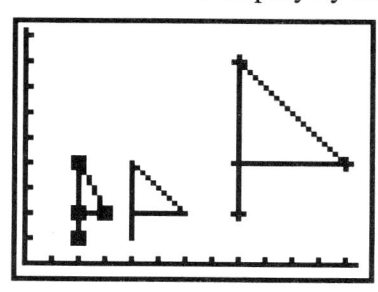

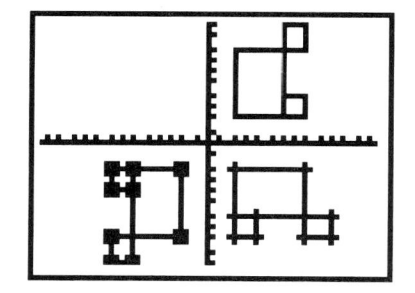

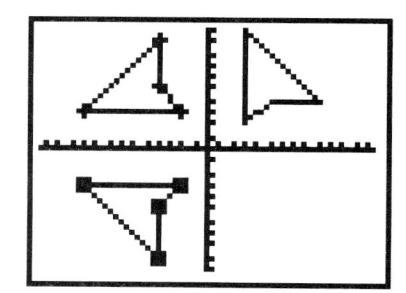

(1) What's the object?

Start by executing program **CLRSCRN** to clear your Graphing screen.

Also clear all the lists, L1 to L6.

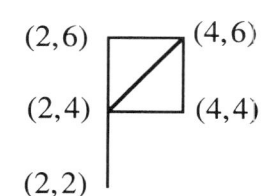

You will need a simple object like this flag. You must be able to draw it without lifting a pen from the paper.

Either use the flag or design a simple shape of your own. Write down its coordinates in sequence and then enter them into lists L1 and L2 like this.

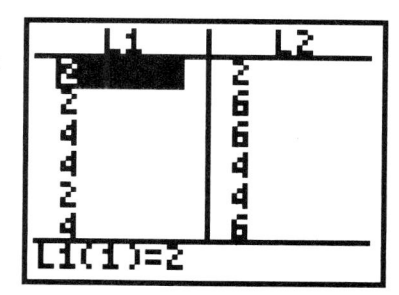

© *Alan Graham and Barrie Galpin*

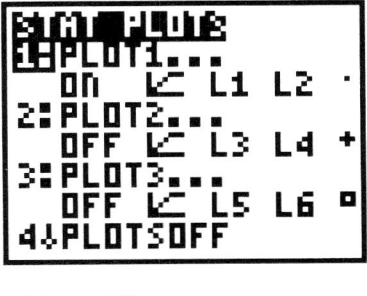

Calculator Maths: Shape

(2) Setting up the plots

Use the [STAT PLOT] key three times to set up three line graphs. Each one should operate on different lists and should use a different mark for the points, as shown here. Notice that PLOT2 and PLOT3 have been set for later use but for the moment they are turned off.

Make sure your Stat Plot menu looks exactly like the one shown here before going any further.

Now execute program **SETSCRN** and you should see your chosen object. If you don't like what you see, go back to the list screen and change the coordinates there until you are happy with your object.

(3) Doing a translation

(a) How would you go about making an image of your object 3 units to the right? The coordinates of the image must go in L3 and L4.
How would you change the X coordinates of the object?
How would you change the Y coordinates of the object?

(b) You need to increase the L1 values by 3 and store them in L3. The values of L2 can be copied directly to L4.

To do this, start on the Home screen and press

[2nd] [L1] [+] 3 [STO▶] [2nd] [L3] [ENTER]
[2nd] [L2] [STO▶] [2nd] [L4] [ENTER]

To turn on PLOT2 press

[2nd] [STAT PLOT] 2 [ENTER]

Press [GRAPH] to see the result.

(c) Press [2nd] [QUIT] [2nd] [ENTRY] [2nd] [ENTRY] and change the **+ 3** to **+ 7**.
Press [ENTER] [GRAPH] and check that the image is as you expected.

(d) Press [2nd] [QUIT] [2nd] [ENTRY] [2nd] [ENTRY] and insert **+ 2** after L2.
What do you expect to see when you press [GRAPH]? Try it and see.
This sort of transformation is called a **translation**.

(e) Experiment for yourself with other translations.
e.g. Try the effect of **L1−3−>L3**.

(4) Double images

(a) Using lists L3 and L4 as above, enter suitable commands on the Home screen to translate the *object* 5 units to the right and 3 units up to produce *Image 1*.

(b) Now enter these two commands to translate *Image 1* 2 units to the right and 4 units down to form *Image 2*.   **L3+2−>L5**   **L4−4−>L6**
Turn on PLOT3 by pressing [2nd] [STAT PLOT] 3 [ENTER] and you should see a display similar to the one at the top of the previous page.

(c) What commands could have been entered which would correspond to translating the *object* onto *Image 2*?

© Alan Graham and Barrie Galpin

Calculator Maths: Shape

(5) Stretching the points

Use a similar method to that used in Activity 3 to investigate the effect of each of the following pairs of commands. In each case write a description of the transformation.

Start with PLOT3 switched off.

(a)   2L1->L3   L2->L4
(b)   .5L1->L3   L2->L4
(c)   L1->L3   1.5L2->L4
(d)   1.5L1->L3   1.5L2->L4

(6) Stretch and translate

(a) Produce this screen display shown here.

To form *Image 1* you need to stretch the X coordinates with factor 2 and leave the Y coordinates unchanged.

To form *Image 2* you need to translate *Image 1* 3 units to the right and 3 up.

(b) Now carry out the same transformations but in the reverse order.

Does *Image 2* turn out to be the same as in part (a)?

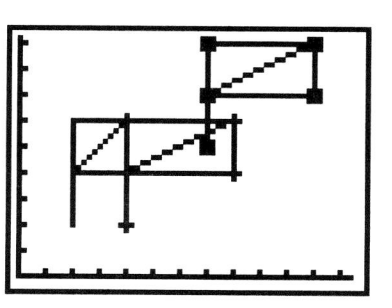

(7) On reflection

Can you predict what transformations each of these commands will produce? Switch off PLOT3 and test your prediction. You may need to change the window settings.

(a)   ⁻L1->L3   L2->L4   (Every X coordinate becomes negative.)
(b)   L1->L3   ⁻L2->L4   (Every Y coordinate becomes negative.)
(c)   ⁻L1->L3   ⁻L2->L4   (All coordinates become negative.)
(d)   L1->L4   L2->L3   (The X and Y coordinates are swapped over.)

(8) Turn and turn again

(a) These two transformations have been drawn using ZDECIMAL window settings.

How do the X coordinates of the *object* relate to the Y coordinates of *Image 1* and vice versa?

How do the X coordinates of the *object* relate to the Y coordinates of *Image 2* and vice versa?

Enter two pairs of commands to produce similar transformations.

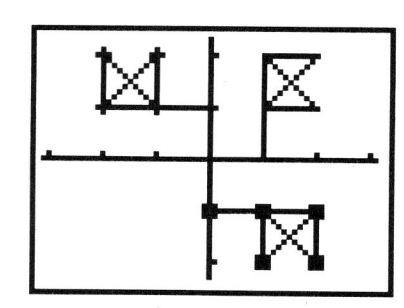

(b) What single transformation would change *Image 1* to *Image 2*?
Can you describe this transformation by referring to what happens to the coordinates?

Enter two commands that would transform the L3 and L4 values into L5 and L6 ones without changing the display above.

© Alan Graham and Barrie Galpin

Calculator Maths: Shape

Brain stretcher   **Matrix transformations**

Sometimes transformations are described using a 2x2 matrix such as $\begin{bmatrix} A & B \\ C & D \end{bmatrix}$.

For example, the matrix $\begin{bmatrix} 2 & 0 \\ 0 & 2 \end{bmatrix}$ represents a transformation you met earlier.

Enter the program **MATFORM** which will enable you to investigate this.

Switch off PLOT3 and execute the program.
Input 2 for A, 0 for B, 0 for C and 2 for D.

You should find that the image is an enlargement, scale-factor 2, centred at the origin.

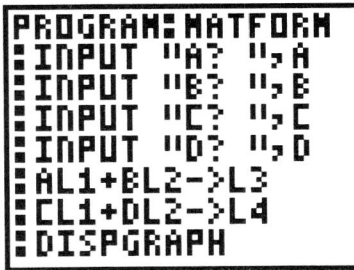

```
PROGRAM:MATFORM
:INPUT "A? ",A
:INPUT "B? ",B
:INPUT "C? ",C
:INPUT "D? ",D
:AL1+BL2→L3
:CL1+DL2→L4
:DISPGRAPH
```

Now investigate the effect of these other matrices.

(a) $\begin{bmatrix} -1 & 0 \\ 0 & 1 \end{bmatrix}$ (b) $\begin{bmatrix} 0 & -1 \\ -1 & 0 \end{bmatrix}$ (c) $\begin{bmatrix} 3 & 0 \\ 0 & .5 \end{bmatrix}$ (d) $\begin{bmatrix} 2 & 1 \\ 0 & 1 \end{bmatrix}$ (e) $\begin{bmatrix} 1 & 0 \\ 0 & 1 \end{bmatrix}$

(f) Experiment with other values and see what transformations you can produce.

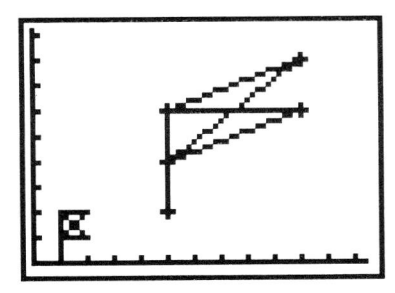

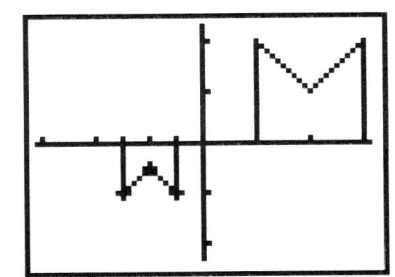

Discussion

- How many different types of transformation have you produced on your calculator?
- How would you recognise a translation? How would you describe it?
- If you combine two translations do you always get another translation? For what other types of transformation is this true?
- What is the difference between a stretch and an enlargement?
- If you reflect in the X axis and then reflect in the Y axis what is the result?
- Does the order in which you carry out two transformations matter?

© Alan Graham and Barrie Galpin

Calculator Maths: Shape *Solutions*

Unit 1
Perimeters and areas

Key ideas
This unit deals with the differences between the perimeter and the area of shapes. The formulas for the perimeter and the area of some simple shapes are used and short calculator programs are developed. The unit includes two well-known investigations which deal with the links between area and perimeter.

Suitable for TI-82 / TI-83? Yes / Yes.

Preparation? You will need to use the program **SETSCRN** from page 26 of **Calculator Maths: Foundations**.

New calculator skills? Use of the programming commands **INPUT** and **DISP**. Use of **GRIDON** and **LINE** from the DRAW menu.

Mathematical jargon used: Perimeter, circumference, formula, trapezium.

Solutions and comments

(1)(a)(d)(h)(i) involve calculating a perimeter.
(b)(c)(e)(f)(g)(j) involve calculating an area.

(2)(a)

	Perimeter	Area
(i)	4L	L^2
(ii)	$2\pi R$	πR^2
(iii)	2W + 2H	WH
(iv)	B + C + D	1/2 BH

All the perimeter formulas involve adding lengths, whereas the areas involve multiplying lengths together.

(3)(a)(i) Perimeter 30 units, area 34 sq. units.
(ii) Perimeter 38 units, area 34 sq. units.
(b)(c) No comments.

Brain stretcher There are 20 and 16 internal points in the two shapes shown. It is possible to find a formula linking P (the perimeter), A (the area) and I (the number of internal points). To find the formula it is best to do some systematic specialisation: e.g. make lots of different shapes with P=12 and find a link between A and I. Then repeat with P=10 and P=8 etc. This should enable you to find a single formula that covers all cases.

(4)(a) You need to use a reasonable estimate for the length of a person's outstretched arms. e.g. If you use a stretch of 170cm the circumference of the tree is about 500cm or 5 metres.
(b) Radius is about 80cm and diameter about 160cm.
(c) Area is about 20 000 sq. cm or 2 sq. m.

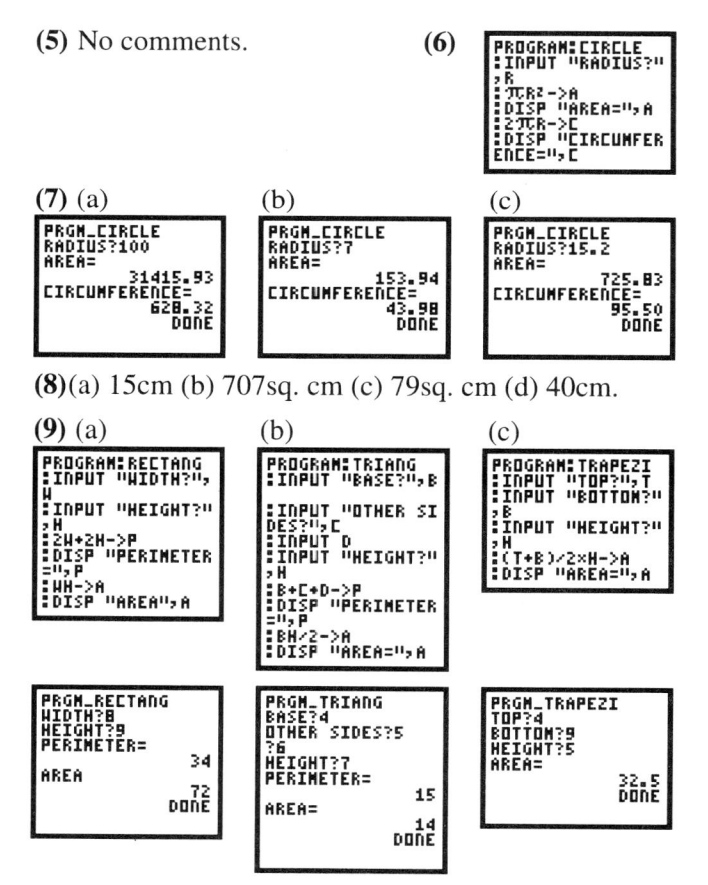

(5) No comments.

(6) [calculator screen: PROGRAM:CIRCLE]

(7) (a) (b) (c) [calculator screens showing PRGM_CIRCLE outputs]

(8)(a) 15cm (b) 707sq. cm (c) 79sq. cm (d) 40cm.

(9) (a) (b) (c) [calculator screens showing PROGRAM:RECTANG, PROGRAM:TRIANG, PROGRAM:TRAPEZI and their outputs]

(10) To calculate the sides you need to subtract the top from 60 and divide by 2. **(60–L1)/2->L2** does this for all the possible top lengths in L1 and stores the answers in L2. Multiplying each value in L1 by its corresponding value in L2 gives the various areas. By investigating the values in L3 you should find that a top length of 20 is not the best option – the maximum enclosed area is actually 450 sq. m. when the top is 30m long.

Discussion

• Perimeters always use units of length like metres, centimetres, inches, miles etc. The corresponding units of area are square metres, square centimetres, square inches, square miles etc.
• A hectare is a square with sides of 100m. 1 hectare =10 000 sq. m. and there are 100 hectares in a sq. kilometre. An acre is an old British unit equivalent to 4840 square yards (or a strip of land 22 yards wide and 220 yards long.) There were 640 acres in a square mile. 1 hectare is about 2.5 acres.
• Just occasionally a shape's area and perimeter may have the same numerical value. E.g. a square with sides 4m long has a perimeter of 16 **metres** and an area of 16 **square metres**.

Solutions   *Calculator Maths: Shape*

Unit 2 Volumes

Key ideas

This unit covers some of the common 3-D shapes, including cube, cuboid, cylinder and cone. You are asked to create your own short programs which calculate the volumes of some of these shapes. This is rather like using the calculator's programming features to create your own calculator button.

Suitable for TI-82 / TI-83? Yes / Yes.

Preparation? It is probably worthwhile, though not essential, to have worked through Unit 1, Perimeters and areas.

New calculator skills? Including one program within another.

Mathematical jargon used: capacity, cuboid, cylinder, cone, sphere.

Solutions and comments

(1)(a) $729mm^3$.
(b) $1.728cm^3$, $512mm^3$, $.216in^3$.
(c) One large cube is equivalent to 8 small ones (i.e. 2×2×2) so Alice needs 24 lumps!

(2)(a) Capacity = $10500cm^3$.
(b) There are 100cm in 1m, 100^2 cm^2 in 1m^2 and 100^3cm^3 in 1m^3. Capacity = $10500 \div 100^3$ = $.0105m^3$.

(3)(a) TI-80 is approx. $208000mm^3$ (163×75×17mm).
TI-82 is approx. $353000 mm^3$ (173×85×24mm).
TI-83 is approx. $367000 mm^3$ (180×85×24mm).
(b) A suitable skeleton program might look like this. Note that the TI-83 allows you to collapse the three separate Input commands using the single command:
    Prompt L,W,H. 
Volume of brick = $1430cm^3$.
A typical classroom might be 12×10×2.5m = $300m^3$.
A typical bath we measured was 140×50×45cm = $315000cm^3$.
(c) A typical cistern we measured was 50×20×20cm = $20 000cm^3$.
No. of flushes = 315 000/20 000 = approx. 16.

(4)(a) 12×12×4cm. Capacity = $576cm^3$.
(b) 16×16×2cm. Capacity = $512cm^3$.
(c) The greatest value is just under 10cm.
(d) Dimensions are: $X \times (20-2X) \times (20-2X)$. Capacity = $X(20-2X)^2$.
(e) The table and graph suggest a maximum capacity when x is around $3^{1}/_{3}$.

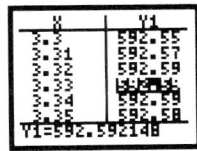

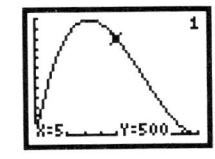

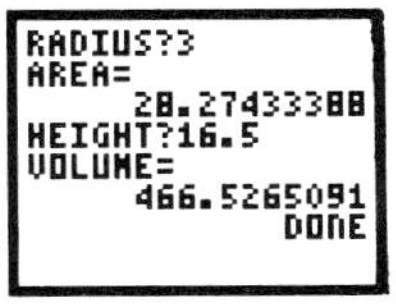

(5) **CYLINDE** should produce a screen rather like this, suggesting a capacity of roughly 467ml.

This is larger than the stated contents for several reasons. For example:
- inaccuracy in measuring the can,
- the can is not an exact cylinder,
- the measurements were of the exterior of the can and capacity refers to internal measurements.

(6)(a) Assuming an outer radius of 5.5cm, an inner radius of 2.3cm and a width of 11.2cm:
Volume of paper = 1064 – 186 = $878cm^3$.
(b) Assuming that each sheet has dimensions 11.2×13.9cm, area of one sheet = 11.2×13.9 cm^2 = $156cm^2$ approx.
Approx. height of pile = 878÷156 = 5.6cm.
(c) Each sheet = 5.6÷280 = .02cm or .2mm.

(7)(a) For A4 sheets, 29.7×21cm.
(b) The short, wide one has the greater capacity.
(c) The radii of the short and tall cylinders are 4.7cm and 3.3cm, respectively. The corresponding capacities are $1474cm^3$ and $1042cm^3$.

(8)(a) Maximum capacity = $102.6cm^3$.
(b) Proportion = 12.8 cm^3 / 102.6 cm^3 = 1/8.
(c) Approx. 79% of the way up the glass (the amount of wine is half the capacity of the glass, so each dimension is scaled by $\sqrt[3]{2}$ (or .79).

Brain stretcher Volume = $417cm^3$.

Discussion

- All cubes are cuboids; not all cuboids are cubes.

- brick, shoe box; baked bean tin; ice cream cone, pencil point, traffic cone.

- Volume is multiplied by 8 (2×2×2).

- Again, volume is multiplied by 8.

- Volume is the amount of space taken up, while capacity is amount of space inside a container.

- A cube is the cuboid with greatest volume for a given surface area.

© *Alan Graham and Barrie Galpin*

Calculator Maths: Shape **Solutions**

Unit 3 Pythagoras' theorem

Key ideas

This unit offers various ways of illustrating the truth of Pythagoras theorem (but not proving it!). Also used is the converse of the theorem (if the three sides of a triangle A, B and C satisfy the expression $A^2 + B^2 = C^2$ then the triangle is right angled.

A second theme is the effect of measurement accuracy on the "truth" of mathematical relationships. Look out for the effect caused by the inevitable inaccuracies when you make measurements.

In Activity 8, there is an investigation of the so-called Pythagorean triples: whole numbers which exactly satisfy the equation $A^2 + B^2 = C^2$. You will have met several examples in earlier activities and are now invited to look for patterns in these numbers.

Three programs are included, two simple ones in Activity 7 and a longer program in Activity 9 which provides experience of estimating diagonal lengths.

Suitable for TI-82 / TI-83? Yes / Yes.

Preparation? Programs from **Calculator Maths: Foundations**, pages 25-6.

New calculator skills? No.

Mathematical jargon used: right-angled triangle (but not hypotenuse).

Solutions and comments

(1) Yes, since $A^2 + B^2 = C^2$. Notice that the converse of Pythagoras' theorem is being used here.

(2) $13.2^2 + 5.8^2 = 207.88$, whereas
$14.5^2 = 210.25$.
You may well feel that this is not (quite) a right-angled triangle. However, this apparent inconsistency is probably just caused by inevitable inaccuracies in the measurements.
For example, if it had been possible to measure the sides to the nearest hundredth of a centimetre you might have got the results shown here – there is still some inconsistency.

(3) Both are examples of Pythagorean triples:
$9^2 + 40^2 = 41^2$
$11^2 + 60^2 = 61^2$.

(4) Do not expect exact results. For example, the labelled triangle has sides of 1.9, 3.8 and 4.3 cm but
$1.9^2 + 3.8^2 = 18.1$
whereas $4.3^2 = 18.5$.

(5) 123.2m. Note the importance of brackets after the square root sign. The screen display shown uses a mode setting of 1 decimal place.
Diagonal of tennis court is 85.9 feet to 1 d.p.

(6) Subtraction is necessary here in order to calculate one of the shorter sides of the triangle. Since sides were given (apparently) correct to the nearest whole number, 46m is a reasonable answer.
The height of the second kite is 84m. Notice another example of a Pythagorean triple:
$13^2 + 84^2 = 85^2$.

(7)(a) The third command calculates the hypotenuse and stores the answer in C.
(b) Here is one possible program. Notice that it could be shortened by replacing the 3rd and 4th lines by
DISP $\sqrt{(C^2 - A^2)}$

(8) So far in this unit you have met the following
3–4–5
9–40–41
11–60–61
13–84–85
Pattern spotting and checking conjectures on the calculator may well produce these other triples:
5–12–13
7–24–25
15–112–113 etc.
The general form of all these is
$2n+1 \quad 2n^2 + 2n \quad 2n^2 + 2n + 1$
where n is a positive integer.
You may also have found multiples of the above such as 6–8–10 etc.

(9) Experience seems to suggest that, when this program is used, estimates improve very rapidly. Changing the window settings and the random integer commands allows a more extensive range of diagonals to be used.
Notice that commands 12 and 13 in the program involve the use of rather complicated trigonometry, so teachers may prefer to use this program on the teacher's calculator with an OHP display.

Discussion

• Yes, the third side can always be calculated, using either addition or subtraction of squares.
• If two sides of a right angled triangle are 5 and 12 units, the other side may be either 13 or 10.9 units. In the first case 5 and 12 were the shortest sides but in the second case 12 was the longest side.
• Activities 2, 4, 5 and 6 should have shown that, when measurements are made of side lengths, Pythagoras' theorem may appear to be only approximately correct. Choosing an appropriate level of accuracy is an important mathematical skill.
• Pythagoras theorem crops up when calculating heights, positioning ladders, finding distances between points on maps etc.

44 © Alan Graham and Barrie Galpin

Solutions *Calculator Maths: Shape*

Unit 4 Sin, cos and tan

Key ideas

This unit introduces the most basic ideas of trigonometry in terms of the ratios of corresponding sides of a right-angled triangle. You will discover for yourself the common ratios represented by several similar right-angled triangles. You are then introduced to the sin, cos and tan keys and the unit ends with a traditional exercise in 'solving' right-angled triangles.

Suitable for TI-82 / TI-83? Yes / Yes.

Preparation? Unit 3, Pythagoras Theorem.

New calculator skills? Use of [SIN] [COS] [TAN] keys and their second functions.

Mathematical jargon used: 'the same shape', trig. ratios, opposite side, adjacent side, hypotenuse.

Solutions and comments

(1)(a) Opposite side = 2.
(b) Adjacent side = 5.
(c) Hypotenuse = 5.4 (to 1 d.p.).
(d) (i) .37.., (ii) .92.., (iii) .4.

(2)(a) Opposite side = 4.
(b) Adjacent side = 10.
(c) Hypotenuse = 10.8 (to 1 d.p.).
(d) (i) .37.., (ii) .92.., (iii) .4.

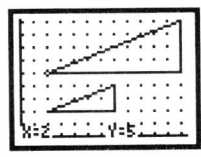

Since the two triangles are the same shape, the ratios of their corresponding sides must be the same. (See Unit 5, Similar shapes.)

(3)(e) The numbers in L3 are the lengths of the hypotenuses of the six triangles.

(4)(a) Because the triangles are similar, the ratios of the corresponding sides will be the same; these ratios correspond to the *sin* of the bottom left angle of the triangle in each case.
(b) For the same reason as in part (a), the ratios of the corresponding sides will be the same; these ratios correspond to the *cos* of the bottom left angle of the triangle in each case.
(c) For the same reason as in part (a), the ratios of the corresponding sides will be the same; these ratios correspond to the *tan* of the bottom left angle of the triangle in each case.

(5)(a) sin 33.7° is approximately the same as the numbers stored in L4 because these values were calculated by dividing the opposite side by the hypotenuse.
(b) Similarly, cos 33.7° is approximately the same as the numbers stored in L5.
(c) Similarly, tan 33.7° is approximately the same as the numbers stored in L6.

(6)(b) The values are displayed below.

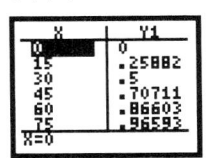

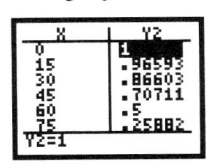

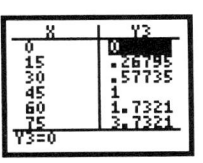

The corresponding values for 90° can be found by scrolling down. They are as follows.
sin 90 = 1, cos 90 = 0, tan 90 produces ERROR.
(c) You may spot that sinX = cos(90−X).
The ERROR message indicates that it is impossible to calculate tan 90.
(d) $\cos^{-1}$ is the inverse function of cos.
(e) $\sin^{-1}$ is the inverse function of sin.
(f) tan 75 = 3.732050808.
The inverse tan of 3.732050808 is 75°.

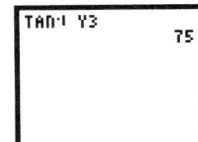

Brain stretcher To produce each of these screens, the cursor must first be positioned on the appropriate value of Y1, Y2 or Y3 in the TABLE screen. Otherwise the method is similar to that used in Activity 6.

(7)(a) A = 6cos 25 = 5.4.
(b) $H^2 = O^2 + A^2 = 36$, which one might expect from Pythagoras Theorem.
(c) QR = 9.8, PQ = 6.9.
(d) (i) XZ = 8.6cm,
(ii) X = 54.5°, Y = 90°, Z = 35.5°.

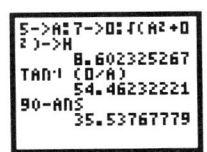

Discussion

• Whereas [SIN], [COS] and [TAN] turn angles of a right-angled triangle into ratios of sides, the second functions do the reverse (they are the inverse functions).

• The largest values of sinX and cosX are 1. However, there is no maximum value of tanX (try for example tan 89°, tan 89.5°, etc.)

• sinX / cosX = tanX.

• Trig. ratios outside the range 0° to 90° can be explored using graphs, tables or Home screen calculations.

• Use Zoom, Option 7 to provide suitable window settings. The graphs are shown here.

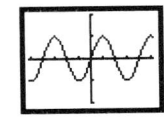

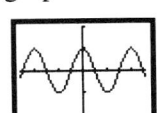

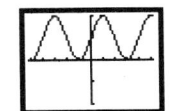

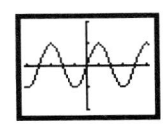

Y= sinX + 1 is basically the standard sine curve shifted up one unit. Y= cos(90−X) is the same graph as Y= sinX – see Activity 6(c).

© Alan Graham and Barrie Galpin

Calculator Maths: Shape — *Solutions*

Unit 5   Similar shapes

Key ideas

This unit deals with two useful ways of describing shapes that look alike; **congruent** shapes are identical in every respect and **similar** shapes have exactly the same shape but one may be larger than the other. Two other key properties of similar shapes are that they have the same angles and the sides are in proportion.

Suitable for TI-82 / TI-83?   Yes / Yes.

Preparation?   No.

New calculator skills?   None.

Mathematical jargon used: Congruent, vertices, similar, proportion, ratio.

Solutions and comments

(1)(a) The vertices are (2,1), (4,2) and (5,6).
(b) The vertices are (6,4), (8,5) and (9,9).
(c) There are several possible answers here, of which this is one.
L1+7->L5
L2->L6

(2) Note: the TI-83 provides a simple command for clearing all the lists (ClrAllLists in MEM). Here is one possibility.
{1,3,3,1,1}->L1
{1,1,2,2,1}->L2
L1+3->L3; L2+3->L4
L1+6->L5; L2+6->L6

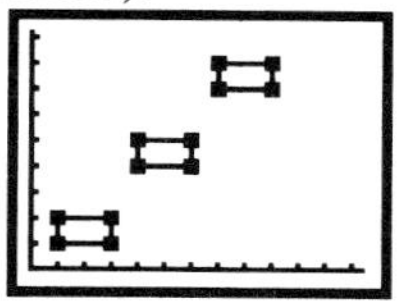

(3)(a) The coordinates of the smaller triangle are (1,2), (3,4) and (6,3). The coordinates of the larger triangle are (2,4), (6,8) and (12,6).
(b) The third triangle shown here was formed using the following commands:

1.5L1->L5: 1.5L2->L6

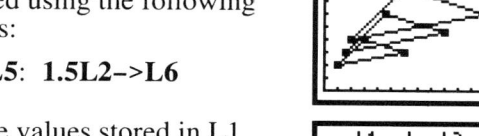

(4)(a) The values stored in L1 and L2 are shown here.
(b) The larger rectangle is formed using **3L1->L3** and **3L2->L4**.

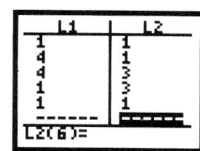

Since the same scaling is used to create the *X* and *Y* coordinates of the larger rectangle, the two rectangles are similar.

(c) Enter **L1/2->L5** and **L2×2->L6**. These two rectangles are not similar because they do not have exactly the same shape.

(5)(a) The rectangle on the left is the odd one out as it is longer and thinner than the proportion of the other two. In fact, the ratio of the sides for the first rectangle is 2.5:1 while the ratio of the sides for the other two is 1.5:1.
(b) As you can see from the screen opposite, the middle rectangle is the odd one out.

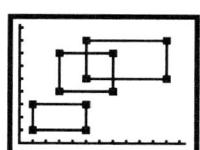

(c) These two rectangles are similar – the ratios of the sides are equal (3:1). Note that two shapes don't have to be the same way round in order for them to be either congruent or similar.

(6)(a) The sides of the larger triangle should be roughly twice as big because it was formed by doubling the coordinates of the smaller triangle.
(b) The ratios might not work out to be exactly as expected due to measuring inaccuracy.

Brain stretcher

This screen shows the values originally stored in L1 and L2. The other lists were formed using:

2L1-7->L3;   2L2-5->L4
3L1-14->L5;   3L2-10->L6

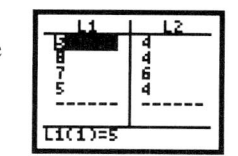

(7)(a) Capacity = 203×93×57 = 1 076 103mm³.
(b) Percentage 'error' =
(1 076 103–1 000 000)/1 000 000 × 100 = 7.6%
(c) New box = $(.9)^3$ of original = .729.
So, reduction = 27% approximately.
(d) If the capacity is multiplied by .5, each dimension must be multiplied by $\sqrt[3]{.5} \approx .79$.
So height of half litre box = .79 × 203 = 160mm.

Discussion

• All squares, circles and equilateral triangles are similar; the others only if they are in proportion.

• For similar triangles, matching angles are equal.

• Dividing length by width for each rectangle gives the same ratio.

• Similar shapes are not necessarily congruent.

• Yes, all congruent shapes are also similar.

• The area increases by a factor of 4 (i.e. 2^2).

• The volume increases by a factor of 8 (i.e. 2^3)

• You can alter its size, position and orientation.

© *Alan Graham and Barrie Galpin*

Unit 6 Locus

Key ideas

Students sometimes find the idea of locus rather tricky but it is given a fairly simple treatment here. Locus is a way of defining a shape by describing the path traced out as you (mentally) move around it.

There are various ways of making such descriptions. In this unit they are largely based on stating the connection between the *X* and *Y* coordinates. The unit should therefore provide a useful revision for work on equations covered in **Calculator Maths**: *Algebra*.

Suitable for TI-82 / TI-83? Yes / Yes.

Preparation? No.

New calculator skills? Use of Y VARS.

Mathematical jargon used: Locus, coordinate, equidistant.

Solutions and comments

(1)(a) No comments.
(b) 6.4516, 12.258, ‑4.516.
(c) 2E‑5, 8.9E‑5, ‑1E‑4.

(2)(a) The coordinates are connected by the rule *Y=X+5*.
(b) **Y1=X+5**.
(c) (-5,0) and (0,5).
(d) Set TBLMIN to .00158 and ΔTBL to .00001.
Press [2nd] [TABLE] to see that the Y value corresponding to X=.00158 is Y=5.00158.

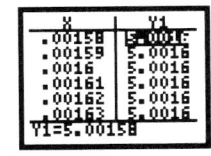

Using a similar method, the other Y values are: Y=5.00063, Y=4.999991.

(3) Each locus, picture and equation is linked as follows:

Locus	Picture	Equation
(a)	(iv)	$Y = 3X - 5$
(b)	(viii)	$Y = 3(X - 5)$
(c)	(v)	$Y = X^2 - 4$
(d)	(i)	$Y = (X - 4)^2$
(e)	(ii)	$Y = 1/X$
(f)	(vii)	$Y = 6$
(g)	(iii)	$Y = 0$
(h)	(vi)	$X = -3$

(4)(a) The dashed line is drawn at Y=4.6. Its locus might be described as: 'a line equidistant from two parallel lines'.
(b) Note that vertical lines cannot be drawn from the Y= screen. Instead, use the command VERTICAL from the Draw menu. The centre line is drawn at X=5.2.

(c) These lines were drawn using **Y1=X+2, Y2=X-4** and **Y3=X-1**.

(d) This 'road' was drawn using:
Y1=10-X
Y2=5-X
Y3=7.5-X

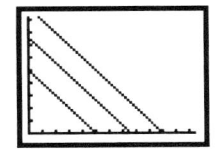

(5) The 8th command of this program is **INPUT** without any store location to follow it. This makes the calculator go to the Graphing screen and wait while you move the cursor. When you press [ENTER] the current values of X and Y are saved. The 9th command tests to see if the distance of (X,Y) from (A,B) is almost the same as from (C,D). At the moment the squares of the distances have to be less than 1 unit but you might try changing this to < 2 or < 3 to see the difference it makes.

(6)(a) The locus is a circle centred at the origin.
(b) and (c) No comments.

Brain stretcher

(a) The locus is the straight line which bisects the right angle where the two points intersect. (There are two such bisecting lines but we shall illustrate only one here.)

(b) The bisector shown here makes an angle of 45° to the horizontal and so will have a gradient of 1 (the other bisector has a gradient of -1). The line must also pass through (4,5), so the equation to use is **Y1=X+1**.

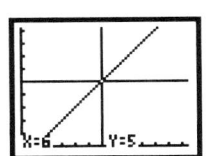

Discussion

• Tie the two poles together. Place one pole in the ground and, keeping the string taut, mark out the circle with the other pole.
The locus of the circle is a path which is a constant distance from a fixed point.

• Tie two poles together. Place them in the ground but apart so that the string is loose. Use the third pole to make the string taut. Keeping the string taut, mark out the ellipse with the third pole.
The locus of the ellipse is a path for which the sum of the distances from two fixed points is constant.

© *Alan Graham and Barrie Galpin*

Calculator Maths: Shape *Solutions*

Unit 7 Polygons

Key ideas

There are two ways of drawing polygons on the graphics calculator but unfortunately both of them make use of rather advanced mathematics. Both use trig. functions and one also uses parametric graphing. We have decided to not to use the parametric method although you may want to try it with more advanced students. In parametric mode you can define X1T=2COS T and Y1T=2SIN T for example, with T values determined in the Window menu.

The alternative approach outlined in Activity 1, uses SEQ to store the coordinates of vertices in lists and a statistical line graph to draw polygons. This allows students to draw different regular polygons and star-like shapes.

In the second half of the unit, students are asked to write short programs which draw polygons line by line. They then use them to draw lots of shapes to produce polyominoes and tessellations.

Suitable for TI-82 / TI-83? Yes / Yes.

Preparation? None.

New calculator skills? Use of INPUT without store location in program. Use of GOTO and LBL.

Mathematical jargon used: Regular polygon, polyominoes (etc.), tessellation.

Solutions and comments

(1) The method used by the calculator is to compute the coordinates of vertices using trig. ratios of angles which are multiples of 72°.

(2) (a) You will see a square but you might not expect this orientation.
(b) The equilateral triangle uses multiples of 120°. The regular heptagon uses multiples of 360/7 or 51°.

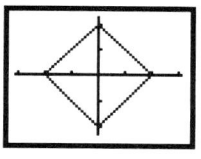

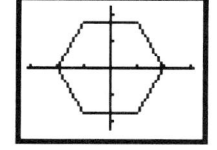

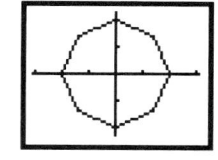

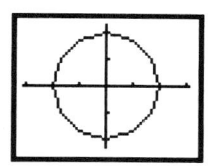

(c) 60°, 45° and 30°.

(3)(a) 4° would produce a 90-sided polygon which appears as a circle on the calculator.

(b) 180° suggests a 2-sided polygon. Tracing reveals the vertices at (2,0) and (-2,0).
(c) 100 is not a factor of 360 so it does not produce a regular polygon.

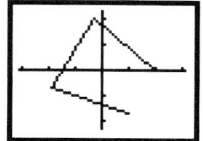

(4) The commands suggested produce the drawing shown here. Other final values in the SEQ commands which produce interesting drawings include: 144, 135, 103, 160.

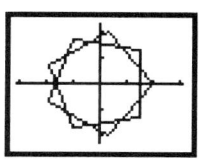

However, values of 36 or less will produce a sequence with too many values to store in L1 and L2 and an Invalid Dim error message appears.

(5) The complete program is shown here.

(6) There are 5 different tetrominoes and 12 different pentominoes as shown below.

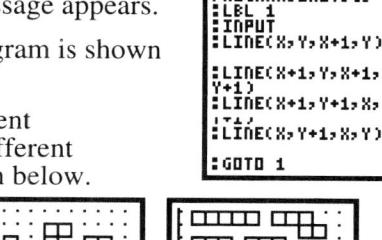

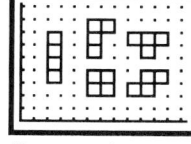

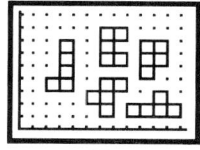

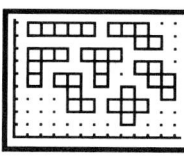

5 tetrominoes   *12 pentominoes*

The pentominoes are quadrilaterals, hexagons and octagons. (Why no odd numbers of sides?) There are two triominoes and only one domino and one monomino.

(7) The octagon does not have equal sides, so it is not regular.
The two tessellations are semi-regular (since they are made up of two shapes, octagons and squares. Note that the two tessellations use two different-sized squares, with sides corresponding to the two different length sides of the octagon.

Brain stretcher The tessellations shown are all regular, since they all use a single shape. They all make use of the unit grid to determine the coordinates of the vertices. A tessellation of regular hexagons is difficult to produce on the graphics calculator: it is hard to define non-integer coordinates because of the resolution of the screen determined by pixel size.

The third tessellation was drawn using a program which produces two of the basic shapes at once.

Discussion

• This unit refers to triangles, various quadrilaterals, pentagons, hexagons, heptagons, octagons, and dodecagons.
• In this unit the only angles used are the angles subtended at the centre by the sides of regular polygons. (i.e. for an *n*-sided polygon the angle is 360° ÷ *n*).
• When n is large, regular polygons resemble circles on the calculator's screen.
• Polyominoes are examples of non-regular polygons (for example, the domino is a rectangle).

Unit 8 Circles

Key ideas

To draw a circle on a graphics calculator requires entering equations which are derived either from Pythagoras' theorem or from trig. ratios. In this unit both approaches are used and to understand the methods you will need to have tackled units 3 and 4 first. Activities 1 to 6 can then provide a way of revising and drawing together trigonometric ideas.

However, in Activity 7 you do not need to draw circles on your calculator, so this activity can be used on its own if you have not studied Pythagoras and trigonometry yet. The activity asks you to measure the circumference and diameter of various circular objects and then use the calculator to analyse the data collected.

Suitable for TI-82 / TI-83? Yes / Yes.

Preparation? Pythagoras' theorem, sin, cos and tan, also, for Activity 1, Squares and square roots from **Calculator Maths:** *Number*.

New calculator skills? Use of parametric graphing.

Mathematical jargon used: radius, circumference, diameter, π, parameter.

Solutions and comments

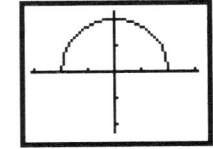

(1)(a) (b) Entering Y2 = ⁻Y1 on the Y= screen produces the negative values and the full circle is drawn.

You might like to try selecting **SIMUL** on the bottom line of the MODE menu. This will cause circles to be produced in a rather more satisfying way.

(2) This activity is designed to help stress the fact that $X^2 + Y^2 = R^2$. For every entry of $X^2 + Y^2$ you should get the value 4 (since in this case R = 2).

Brain stretcher

The display in the unit was produced using this program.

```
PROGRAM:BULLSI
:CLRDRAW
:FOR(R,0,4,.5)
:DRAWF Y1
:DRAWF Y2
:END
```

(3) In parametric graphing each pair of X and Y coordinates is calculated from another variable (or parameter), in this case T, the angle at the centre of the circle. The values of T are set to start at 0 and go up to 360 so the points of the circle are drawn in a different order, starting on the right hand side and proceeding anticlockwise.

(4) This is a repeat of Activity 2 using the alternative specification for the circle. Again $X^2 + Y^2$ will be 4 (=R^2).

(5) To produce the eyes and the nose the Y= screen should be as shown here, with 1 stored in R.

(e) Here are some possible faces, with embellishments using the LINE option from the draw menu.

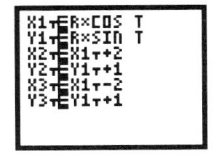

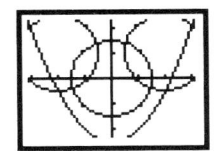

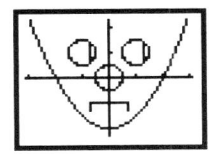

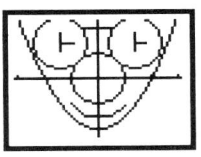

(6) No comments.

(7) The success of this activity will depend upon how accurately you measure the circumference and diameter of the various objects. Using the values given in the unit produces the screen displays shown below.

The values in L3 should be close to or a little above 3.

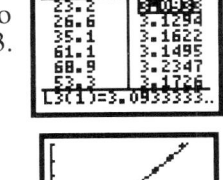

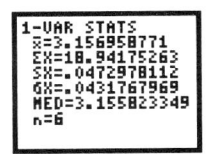

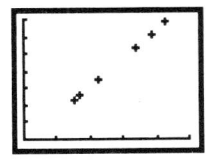

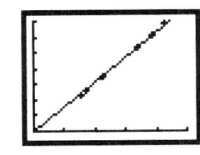

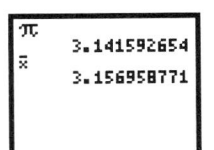

(h) The circumference (C) of a circle is π times its diameter (D). So C = πD.
(i) The circumference (C) of a circle is 2π times its radius (R). So C = 2πR.

Discussion

• A circle is defined in the unit as the set of points which are the same distance from the centre point (i.e. just the points *on* the line). However, we often speak of the area *of* a circle rather than the area *inside* a circle and this would imply that the points inside are part of the circle too!
• This is a further opportunity to discuss the two alternative ways of representing a circle.
• You may want to discuss the nature of the number π. It is an irrational number; that is it cannot be expressed as a fraction. 22/7 is a reasonable approximation but is not equal to π.
• If the radius is doubled, the circumference is also doubled, but the area become four times what it was.

© Alan Graham and Barrie Galpin

Calculator Maths: Shape   *Solutions*

Unit 9 Transforming shapes

Key ideas

In this unit you will use the calculator to illustrate various simple transformations. The approach used here is to apply simple arithmetic operations to X and Y coordinates and to see the geometric effect.
Adding or subtracting a constant to the coordinates gives rise to translations. Multiplying and dividing by a constant gives rise to stretches and enlargements. Changing the sign gives rise to a reflection in an axis; exchanging the X and Y coordinates to a reflection in $Y=X$, etc.

Suitable for TI-82 / TI-83? Yes / Yes. The matrix-handling facilities of the TI-83 make this topic even more accessible with that machine and different approaches are possible.

Preparation? Plotting coordinates in **Calculator Maths:** *Algebra*.

New calculator skills? No.

Mathematical jargon used: object, image, translation, stretch, enlargement, scale factor, reflection, rotation.

Solutions and comments

(1) If you design your own shape you would be well advised to keep it very simple. Ideally the shape should not be symmetrical and coordinates should lie within the range 0 to 6.

(2) It is essential at this stage that PLOT2 and PLOT3 are turned off, otherwise, as lists L3 to L6 hold no values, a STAT PLOT error will occur.

(3) The procedure for creating images is spelled out in some detail here. In later activities you are expected to be able to use this procedure without help.

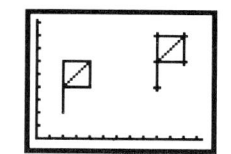

Note the important press of ENTER once the previous line has been edited in part (c).

(4)(a) L1+3–>L3 L2+2–>L4
(b) No comments (c) L1+7–>L5 L2-1–>L6
This is an important idea. The two original translations can be combined into a single 'short cut'.

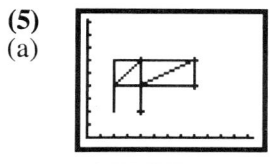

(5)
(a) This is a one-way stretch in the X direction, stretch factor 2. Every point is twice as far from the Y axis as it was.

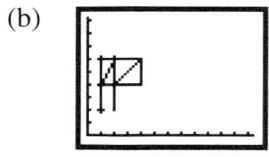

(b) A one-way stretch in the X direction, stretch factor 0.5. Every point is half as far from the Y axis as it was.

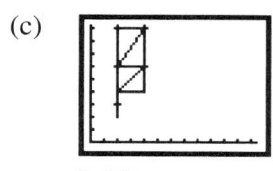

(c) A one-way stretch in the Y direction, stretch factor 1.5. Every point is 1.5 times as far from the X axis as it was.

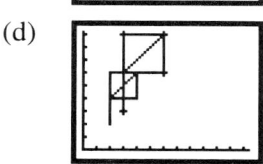

(d) A two-way stretch with stretch factor 1.5 in both directions – normally described as an enlargement, scale factor 1.5. Every point is 1.5 times as far from both axes as it was.
This means that the distance of every point from the origin is 1.5 times what it was.

(6) Reversing the order of the transformations produces a different result. Usually combining transformations is not commutative. (i.e. the order matters!)

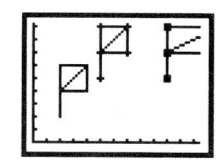

(7)(a) Reflection in the Y axis.
(b) Reflection in the Y axis.
(c) Either two reflections in the axes, or a rotation of 180° about the origin.
(d) Reflection in the line $Y=X$.

(8)(a) L1–>L4 and ⁻L2–>L3 produce the rotation of 90° anticlockwise. ⁻L1–>L6 and L2–>L5 produce the rotation of 90° clockwise.
(b) A rotation of 180°. Both sets of coordinates have their signs changed. ⁻L3–>L5 and ⁻L4–>L6.

Brain stretcher An explanation of matrices and how they may be used to describe transformations is beyond the scope of this book.
(a) Reflection in the Y axis.
(b) Reflection in the line $Y=⁻X$.
(c) A 2-way stretch, scale factor 3 in the X direction and 0.5 in the Y direction.
(d) A shear with invariant $Y=⁻1$ mapping (1,1) to (3,1).
(e) The identity matrix, mapping the object onto itself.

Discussion

• Translations, stretches, enlargements, reflections, rotations, (and others in the Brain stretcher).
• Translations preserve the orientation and size. Describe them by distance and direction moved, or using X and Y movements.
• Two translations always produce another translation. True also for stretches, enlargements and rotations (about the same centre), but not for reflections.
• Enlargement is a 2-way stretch with the same factors in both directions.
• Equivalent to a rotation of 180°.
• Generally the order does make a difference though there are many exceptions to this rule.

© *Alan Graham and Barrie Galpin*